GODS 21ST CENTURY MIGHTY MEN

The Path to Becoming Soldiers in the Army of God

Dr Michael H Yeager

(Some of the teaching in this book is partly taken from the Adam Clarke Commentary, and other non-copy right material found on the internet)

ISBN: 9798862714746

DEDICATION

All of the Scriptures used in this book on **"Gods Mighty Men"** is from the original 1611 version of the King James Bible. I give thanks to God the Father, Jesus Christ, and the Holy Ghost for the powerful impact the word has had upon my life. Without the word Quickened in my heart by the Holy Ghost I would've been lost and undone. To the Lord of Heaven and Earth I am eternally indebted for his great love and his mercy, his protections and his provisions, his divine guidance and overwhelming goodness, the **Price He PAID for His Glorious Church**! To him be glory and praise for ever and ever: Amen.

CONTENTS

ACKNOWLEDGMENTS

*To our heavenly Father and His wonderful love.

*To our Lord, Savior and Master — Jesus Christ, Who saved us and set us free because of His great love for us.

*To the Holy Spirit, Who leads and guides us into the realm of truth and miraculous living every day.

*To all of those who had a part in helping me get this book ready for the publishers.

*To my Lovely Wife, and our precious children, Michael, Daniel, Steven, Stephanie, Catherine Yu, who is our precious daughter-in-law, and Naomi, who is now with the Lord.

Important Introduction

In this teaching book, I will also present a collection of authentic supernatural experiences and testimonies that I have personally witnessed and encountered, as well as those from my family, fellow church members, and others. These miraculous events have been recounted and shared to the best of my ability, but they represent only a small portion of the countless supernatural and divine miracles we have experienced throughout our lives.

Indeed, as the Bible states in **John 21:25 , "And there are also many other things which Jesus did, the which, if they should be written every one, I suppose that even the world itself could not contain the books that should be written. Amen."**

The stories I am about to share with you in this volume represent merely a selection of the most remarkable and memorable moments we have been blessed to experience in our journey with the Lord. Some of these accounts may seem astonishing or even implausible, but I assure you, they are all true. As the Scripture declares in **Luke 1:37 , "For with God nothing shall be impossible."** This book is not intended as a testament to our spirituality, but rather as a tribute to the boundless love and power of the Father, the Son, and the Holy Ghost.

In sharing these extraordinary experiences, I have done my utmost to accurately convey my recollections and understanding of the events. However, it is important to note that not every conversation recounted in these pages is an exact, word-for-word transcription. As it is written in **2 Timothy 3:16-17 , "All scripture is given by inspiration of God, and is profitable for doctrine, for reproof, for correction, for instruction in righteousness: That the man of God may be perfect, thoroughly furnished unto all good works."**

CHAPTER ONE

David and His Mighty Men: Pillars of Faith and Valor in Ancient Israel

The biblical narrative presents numerous figures of faith and courage, but few captivate the imagination as David does. **His** single-handed defeat of Goliath is a testament to his faith in the Almighty. This triumph was not just a personal victory for David, but it sowed seeds of inspiration, rallying others to rise up in faith and might.

"And David said to Saul, Let no man's heart fail because of him; thy servant will go and fight with this Philistine." - 1 Samuel 17:32 (KJV)

The aftermath of his confrontation with Goliath laid the foundation for David's ascendancy as a leader, drawing to him men from various walks of life, particularly those in distress, debt, or bitterness of soul.

"And everyone that was in distress, and everyone that was in debt, and everyone that was discontented, gathered themselves unto him; and he became a captain over them: and there were with him about four hundred men." - 2 Samuel 22:1-2 (KJV)

Running from the wrath of King Saul, David found himself at the helm of a group of men who, though disparate in their backgrounds, found unity under his leadership. Their collective experience, shaped by adversity and kindled by faith, would form the core of what became known as "The **Mighty Men**" or "The Thirty."

The prowess and valor of the **Mighty Men** are well documented in the Scriptures, particularly in 2 Samuel 23:8-39 and 1 Chronicles 11:10-47. These were not merely warriors; they were paragons of bravery, symbols of unwavering loyalty, and embodiments of faith.

"These be the names of the Mighty Men whom David had: The Tachmonite that sat in the seat, chief among the captains; the same was Adino the Eznite: he lift up his spear against eight hundred, whom he slew at one time." - 2 Samuel 23:8 (KJV)

The narrative details more than just thirty individuals, with 2 Samuel 23 concluding that there were thirty-seven in total. Within this prestigious group, a trio emerged as particularly distinguished:

Josheb-Basshebeth, a Tahkemonite, who famously wielded his spear against eight hundred enemies in a single encounter.

Eleazar, son of Dodo the Ahohite, recognized for his valor in standing his ground and striking down Philistines until his hand grew weary.

Shammah, son of Agee the Hararite, who defended a plot of lentils from the Philistines, standing firm and securing a significant victory.

In essence, David's **Mighty Men** were not just remarkable for their physical feats on the battlefield, but also for their spiritual fortitude. Their unity, bravery, and undying loyalty to David were underpinned by a shared faith in **God**, mirroring David's own unwavering trust in the Divine.

The story of David and his **Mighty Men** is a timeless tale of faith, leadership, and valor. It serves as a potent reminder of the transformative power of faith, both on an individual and collective level. David's faith empowered him to face Goliath, and in turn, his leadership and belief inspired a group of distressed, indebted, and discontented men to rise above their challenges and become **Mighty** in **God**. Their legacy is not just one of physical strength and battlefield victories but is firmly rooted in the unshakeable faith and trust in the Almighty.

The Exemplary Qualities of David: A Reflection on Godly Virtues

King David, who was a type and shadow of **Jesus Christ**, was also a central figure in the scriptures of the Old Testament. **He** has long been revered not only for his earthly achievements but more so for his spiritual character. David's relationship with **God** was one of depth and intimacy, reflecting a life lived in surrender and devotion. This teaching aims to elucidate twenty-three distinct qualities of David, as depicted in the Holy Bible, KJV.

1. A Heart after God

One of David's most significant qualities was his deep yearning for **God**. **His** passion and thirst for the divine set him apart. This profound connection and intimacy made him the 'man after **God's** own heart.'

2. Obedience to God

David exemplified obedience. Even in the face of challenges, he consistently sought to align his actions with **God's** will.

3. Perception: Seeing as God Sees

David's vision transcended human understanding. **He** recognized the importance of unity in **God's** eyes, as depicted in the phrase, "if two be not agreed together."

4. Faith, Trust, and Confidence in God

David's unwavering faith is evident in his words, **"And David said to Saul, Let no man's heart fail because of him; thy servant will go and fight with this Philistine." (1 Samuel 17:32). He** further declares, **"The LORD is my rock, and my fortress, and my deliverer; my God, my strength, in whom I will trust; my buckler, and the horn of my salvation, and my high tower." (Psalm 18:2).**

5. Reverence: The Fear of the Lord

David maintained a healthy reverence for the **Lord**, recognizing **His** power and authority in every situation.

6. Love for God and His Word
David cherishes **God's** teachings, declaring, **"The law of the LORD is perfect, converting the soul: the testimony of the LORD is sure, making wise the simple." (Psalm 19:7).**

7. Courage in the Face of Adversity
David's confrontation with Goliath is a testament to his courage. **He** declares, **"Then said David to the Philistine, Thou comest to me with a sword, and with a spear, and with a shield: but I come to thee in the name of the LORD of hosts, the God of the armies of Israel, whom thou hast defied." (1 Samuel 17:45).**

8. Humility: Recognizing One's Place
Despite his triumphs, David remained humble, questioning, **"And David said, Who am I? and what is my life, or my father's family in Israel, that I should be son in law to the king?" (1 Samuel 18:18).**

9. Repentance: A Heart that Seeks Forgiveness
David, realizing his transgressions, earnestly prayed, **"Create in me a clean heart, O God; and renew a right spirit within me." (Psalm 51:10).**

10. Loyalty: Devotion Beyond Boundaries
David's loyalty extends beyond personal ties, as seen when he asks, **"And David said, Is there yet any that is left of the house of Saul, that I may shew him kindness for Jonathan's sake?" (2 Samuel 9:1).**

11. Deep Devotion to God
David's adoration is captured in the words, **"O LORD, our Lord, how excellent is thy name in all the earth!" (Psalm 8:9).**

12. Worship and Praise from the Depths
David danced before **God, "And David danced before the LORD with all his might; and David was girded with a linen ephod." (2 Samuel 6:14),** exemplifying a heart overflowing with joy and gratitude.

13. Mercy: Compassion in Action
Even when wronged, David chose mercy, stating, **"And David said to Abishai, Destroy him not: for who can stretch forth his hand against the LORD'S anointed, and be guiltless?" (1 Samuel 26:9).**

14. Seeking God's Guidance
David consistently sought divine direction, **"And David enquired at the LORD, saying, Shall I pursue after this troop? shall I overtake them? And he answered him, Pursue: for thou shalt surely overtake them, and without fail recover all." (1 Samuel 30:8).**

15. A Heart filled with Thankfulness
David expressed gratitude wholeheartedly, **"I will praise thee, O LORD, with my whole heart; I will shew forth all thy marvellous works." (Psalm 9:1).**

16. Endurance in Trials
In times of distress, David's faith was his anchor, **"I had fainted, unless I had believed to see the goodness of**

the LORD in the land of the living." (Psalm 27:13).

17. A Desire for Righteousness

David prayed, **"Lead me, O LORD, in thy righteousness because of mine enemies; make thy way straight before my face." (Psalm 5:8)**, revealing his yearning for upright living.

18. Generosity: A Giving Spirit

David's generosity shone as he declared, **"Moreover, because I have set my affection to the house of my God, I have of mine own proper good, of gold and silver, which I have given to the house of my God, over and above all that I have prepared for the holy house." (1 Chronicles 29:3).**

19. Compassion and Understanding

David's heart ached with compassion, as seen when he enquired about his child, **"But when David saw that his servants whispered, David perceived that the child was dead: therefore David said unto his servants, Is the child dead? And they said, He is dead." (2 Samuel 12:19).**

20. Dependence on God

David knew his strength came from the **Lord**, **"In the day when I cried thou answeredst me, and strengthenedst me with strength in my soul." (Psalm 138:3).**

21. Zeal for God's Honor

David's zeal for **God** was unwavering, **"The zeal of thine house hath eaten me up; and the reproaches of**

them that reproached thee are fallen upon me." (Psalm 69:9).

22. Fellowship with God
David's deepest desire was to be with the **Lord**, **"One thing have I desired of the LORD, that will I seek after; that I may dwell in the house of the LORD all the days of my life, to behold the beauty of the LORD, and to enquire in his temple." (Psalm 27:4).**

23. Longing for God's Touch
David's soul longed for **God** as fervently as **"As the hart panteth after the water brooks, so panteth my soul after thee, O God." (Psalm 42:1).**

The life of David, as chronicled in the scriptures, provides us with a rich tapestry of virtues to emulate. Each quality embodies a dimension of spiritual maturity and depth, inviting every believer to strive for such an intimate relationship with **God**. From unwavering faith to profound humility, David's attributes serve as pillars for a life dedicated to serving the Divine.

David's heart, always attuned to **God**, was the bedrock of his character. Even when he faltered, his willingness to repent and turn back to **God** set him apart. **His** life was not without its challenges, yet through every trial and triumph, his dependency on **God** remained steadfast. **His** songs and prayers, many of which are encapsulated in the Psalms, continue to inspire countless believers across generations, reminding us of the profound beauty of a life lived in complete surrender to **God's** will.

In our own spiritual journeys, reflecting upon these exemplary qualities of David offers valuable insights. It encourages us to seek a deeper relationship with our Creator, to be brave in the face of adversity, to remain humble in times of triumph, and to continuously yearn for **God's** presence in our lives.

May the legacy of David's relationship with **God** inspire and challenge us to cultivate these virtues in our own lives, drawing us ever closer to the heart of the Divine. And in doing so, may we too become individuals after **God's** own heart.

A Man After God's Own Heart:

David is described as a man after **God's** own heart **(1 Samuel 13:14; Acts 13:22).** Despite his flaws, he had a unique relationship with **God**.

Goliath's Slayer:
As a young boy, he defeated the giant Goliath using just a sling and a stone (1 Samuel 17).
This victory highlighted his faith in **God** and courage.

Talented Musician:
David was a skilled harpist.
He played the harp to soothe King Saul during his troubled times (1 Samuel 16:23).

Prolific Psalmist:
Many of the Psalms in the Bible are attributed to David. **His** writings showcase deep spirituality, anguish, joy, and faith.

King of Israel:
David was the second king of Israel after Saul.
He reigned for 40 years, marking a golden age for Israel.

Established Jerusalem:
David captured the city of Jerusalem from the Jebusites.
He made it the political and religious center of Israel.

Unifying Force:
David united the fragmented tribes of Israel.
He transformed them into a single cohesive nation.

Messianic Lineage:
The Bible says **Jesus Christ** is a descendant of David. Prophecies point to a "Messiah" from David's line (Matthew 1:1).

Dramatic Personal Life:
David had an adulterous relationship with Bathsheba.
He plotted to have her husband, Uriah, killed in battle (2 Samuel 11).

Family Strife:
David faced rebellion from his son Absalom.
Absalom temporarily drove David out of Jerusalem (2 Samuel 15-18).

Repentant Sinner:

David showed profound remorse after his sin with Bathsheba.
He wrote Psalm 51 as a deep expression of repentance.

Mighty Warriors:
David had "David's **Mighty Men**," loyal warriors who excelled in battle (2 Samuel 23).
These warriors performed astonishing feats for him.

Ark of the Covenant:
David brought the Ark of the Covenant to Jerusalem.
This act reaffirmed Israel's worship of Yahweh (2 Samuel 6).

Prophetic Role:
Some of David's Psalms are considered Messianic prophecies.
They point to events in the life, death, and resurrection of **Jesus**.

Military Conquests:
David expanded Israel's borders significantly.
He established control over vast territories.

King David's life was a blend of triumphs and tragedies, faithfulness, and failings. Yet through it all, his commitment to **God**, his raw honesty in expressing both joys and sorrows, and his significant impact on the nation of Israel make his story one of the most compelling in the Bible.

David's Mighty Men: Loyalty in Times of Rejection and Persecution

The scripture paints a vivid picture of King David's journey from being a persecuted shepherd boy to becoming one of the greatest kings in Israel's history. Central to this journey are the individuals who recognized the divine anointing upon David, even when the majority turned against him. These individuals, often referred to as David's **Mighty Men**, offer timeless lessons on loyalty, discernment, and the significance of aligning oneself with **God's** anointed.

In the book of 1 Chronicles chapter 12, the chronicler enumerates those who supported David during his period of distress, **"And these were the numbers of the bands that were ready armed to the war, and came to David to Hebron, to turn the kingdom of Saul to him, according to the word of the LORD." (1 Chronicles 12:23 KJV).** Supporting David during these tumultuous times was not an easy choice, for David, although anointed, was not yet the established king.

The Christian journey draws a parallel with this narrative. Believers are called to live for the **Lord** wholeheartedly, not just in the afterlife but here on earth, where righteousness is often despised and rejected. **Jesus** Himself emphasized this in the Gospel of Luke: **"Woe unto you, when all men shall speak well of you! for so did their fathers to the false prophets. Blessed are ye, when men shall hate you, and when they shall separate you from their company, and shall reproach**

you, and cast out your name as evil, for the Son of man's sake." (Luke 6:26-22 KJV). Recognizing and standing by the truth often requires going against the tide of popular opinion.

Paul the Apostle, one of the stalwarts of the Christian faith, experienced rejection and abandonment during his ministry. Despite his unwavering commitment to the gospel, he lamented, **"This thou knowest, that all they which are in Asia be turned away from me; of whom are Phygellus and Hermogenes." (2 Timothy 1:15 KJV).** Yet, in the midst of adversity, Paul held steadfast, teaching us that the journey with **Christ**, much like David's journey to kingship, is not without its challenges.

David's encounter with the sons of Benjamin in 1 Chronicles 12:16 also underscores the importance of discernment. Upon their arrival, David said, **"If ye come peaceably unto me to help me, mine heart shall be knit unto you: but if ye come to betray me to mine enemies, seeing there is no wrong in mine hands, the God of our fathers look thereon, and rebuke it." (1 Chronicles 12:17 KJV).** This narrative illustrates the necessity for believers to be vigilant, discerning between genuine allies and potential betrayers, and relying on **God's** judgment.

The story of David's **Mighty Men** serves as a potent reminder that loyalty, discernment, and the courage to stand by **God's** anointed, even in times of adversity, are qualities that are eternally cherished by **God**. These men teach us that genuine recognition of **God's** anointing is not based on the prevailing circumstances but on an unwavering commitment to **God's** purpose. As modern-day believers, we are encouraged to emulate the faithfulness of David's **Mighty Men**, standing firm in our convictions and always seeking alignment with **God's** divine plan.

Mighty Men in the Bible: Recognizing the Anointing and Valuing Fellowship

The Bible, time and again, presents stories of men who stood valiantly for **God**, not necessarily by their strength or wisdom, but through the discernment of the Holy Spirit's anointing upon them. These individuals provide significant insights into what it truly means to be a man of **God**.

Take for instance the impactful moment involving Amasai in **1 Chronicles 12:18**. The (KJV) states: **"Then the spirit came upon Amasai, who was chief of the captains, and he said, Thine are we, David, and on thy side, thou son of Jesse: peace, peace be unto thee, and peace be to thine helpers; for thy God helpeth thee. Then David received them, and made them captains of the band."** Amasai, one of David's thirty valiant men, recognized the anointing upon David. This recognition was not based on David's reputation or strength but was a discernment given by the Holy Spirit.

Similarly, church history has shown us that truly Godly individuals often faced persecution from established religious systems. Martin Luther's challenge to the

Roman Catholic doctrines is well known. Yet, lesser-known are the Anabaptists. These devoted followers of **Christ** experienced persecution, not just from Catholics, but even from followers of Martin Luther and John Calvin. Their commitment to **Godliness** and separation from worldly pursuits brought them severe affliction. Despite their challenges, they remained steadfast in their faith. Their story may not be prominent in many church history texts, but their legacy will surely be revealed in the kingdom of heaven.

Another remarkable lesson from David's life can be observed in **1 Chronicles 13:1** (KJV), which says: **"And David consulted with the captains of thousands and hundreds, and with every leader."** This demonstrates the importance of fellowship and consultation in leadership. David, despite his kingship, knew the value of gathering opinions, working in unity, and making collective decisions. This collaborative attitude garnered him immense respect and support from his people, as seen in verse **4: "And all the congregation said that they would do so: for the thing was right in the eyes of all the people."**

The Bible and church history showcase countless **Mighty Men**, not just by their valor or supernatural abilities, but through their discernment of **God's** anointing and their commitment to fellowship and unity. As believers, it is crucial to recognize **God's** anointing on individuals and value the insights of those around us. By doing so, we ensure that our journey of faith is not just about individual accomplishments, but a collective endeavor to glorify **God**.

David's Mighty Men and Their New Testament Counterparts: Lessons on Overcoming

In the scriptures, we find a story in 2 Chronicles about David's three **Mighty Men**. The narrative shares that these men came across a barley field controlled by the Philistines. While all of Israel retreated, not desiring to combat for it, these three champions of David recognized the worth of this field. They were unwavering in their determination to possess it, risking their lives in the process.

"And the Philistines had yet war again with Israel; and David went down, and his servants with him, and fought against the Philistines..." (2 Chronicles 8:13 KJV)

Through their bravery, they garnered **God's** attention, which led to a victorious delivery from the Philistines, granting them the coveted barley field. This field, in spiritual terms, symbolizes our salvation and our identity as over-comers, distinguishing us from Christians contented with mere status quo. We must recognize the value of this "barley field", be willing to defend it, so that **God** might defend and grant it alongside us.

Paul in his first letter to the Corinthians mentioned that events in the Old Testament serve as examples for the New Testament.

"Now all these things happened unto them for examples: and they are written for our admonition,

upon whom the ends of the world are come." (1 Corinthians 10:11 KJV)

The Philistines can be likened to the powers of darkness, adversaries of our souls. Our Promised Land, therefore, is our souls, which the enemy seeks to inhabit. Yet, **God** wishes to reclaim our souls. By gifting us with the Holy Spirit, we are empowered to conquer and reclaim our souls with **His** guidance.

The epiphany I had was that the trio of **Mighty Men** mirrored three apostles in the New Testament. These apostles were taken by **Jesus** to a high mountain, witnessing **His** transfiguration. They epitomize over-comers chosen to reign with **Him.**

Peter: Through his epistles, Peter taught about enduring suffering with faith to overcome.

"That the trial of your faith, being much more precious than of gold that perisheth, though it be tried with fire, might be found unto praise and honour and glory at the appearing of Jesus Christ:" (1 Peter 1:7 KJV)

John: The beloved disciple preached about LOVE and FAITH as tools for overcoming.

"For whatsoever is born of God overcometh the world: and this is the victory that overcometh the world, even our faith." (1 John 5:4 KJV)

James: The **Lord**'s brother instructed about taming our

tongue and being obedient to **God's** will, combining faith with actions to conquer.

"But be ye doers of the word, and not hearers only, deceiving your own selves." (James 1:22 KJV)

David, in his quest, took over Jebus, the most formidable stronghold of their foes. **He** chose to reside there, growing stronger. This stronghold became Jerusalem, **God's** chosen place. The intense battle for Jerusalem is mirrored in the battles for our souls.

"In Salem also is his tabernacle, and his dwelling place in Zion." (Psalm 76:2 KJV)

The path of faith is narrow, demanding effort. Many may aspire but falter due to laziness or worldly desires. But the story of David's **Mighty Men** and their New Testament counterparts shows that with determination, faith, and the right attitude, it's possible to overcome and be in **God's** company. Just as David's men saw the worth of the barley field and stood to fight for it, we too should recognize and battle for our spiritual inheritance. In this journey, may we emerge as valiant warriors, resembling David's **Mighty Men**, and conquer to the very end.

David's Mighty Men and the Giants of Today

David's **Mighty Men** (2 Samuel 21:18-22)

"And it came to pass after this, that there was again a

battle with the Philistines at Gob: then Sibbechai the Hushathite slew Saph, which was of the sons of the giant. And there was again a battle in Gob with the Philistines, where Elhanan the son of Jaare-oregim, a Bethlehemite, slew the brother of Goliath the Gittite, the staff of whose spear was like a weaver's beam. And there was yet a battle in Gath, where was a man of great stature, that had on every hand six fingers, and on every foot six toes, four and twenty in number; and he also was born to the giant. And when he defied Israel, Jonathan the son of Shimeah the brother of David slew him. These four were born to the giant in Gath, and fell by the hand of David, and by the hand of his servants" (2 Samuel 21:18-22 KJV).

This historical recounting of the deeds of David's **Mighty Men** serves to illustrate an imperative spiritual lesson for the believers of today.

A corporate answer to the enemy's challenge is seen when David, the sole warrior, conquers Goliath. It heralds David's initial steps towards the throne for which he was anointed. Now, as the scripture moves forward, we witness a team of **Mighty Men** combating these giants. This transition from individual to corporate combat is symbolic of the broader challenge faced by the Church, as described in Ephesians 6:10-12. The initial battle against the chief giant, Goliath, is now directed against his progenies, representing the manifold challenges that believers face daily.

David's **Mighty Men** are emblematic not of a specific class, but of a spiritual disposition. It is this spirit, a burning devotion to David, that distinguishes them. It's noted in **1 Samuel 17:24 KJV, "And all the men of Israel, when they saw the man, fled from him, and were sore afraid."** The undeterred spirit of these **Mighty Men** contrasts the fear that plagued others when confronted by Goliath. Their unwavering love for David and their recognition of his **God**-ordained role as the King showcases the depth of their commitment.

They were committed not just for personal interests but for a greater cause - the establishment of **God's** ordained king. Just as David's **Mighty Men** were devoted to him and his divine destiny, believers are called to commit to **Christ**. For **Christ** is not just a savior, but also the chosen one by **God**, destined to rule the universe for eternity.

To draw a parallel to the present, it's crucial to understand that faith should not be centered around personal benefits or blessings. It should instead be rooted in the understanding of **God's** larger plan and the role of **Christ** in it. When challenges (or giants) arise, the commitment of believers should not waver or falter. Just as David's **Mighty Men** stood firm, so should modern-day believers stand united and strong in their faith, brushing aside personal fears or concerns.

In , the saga of David's **Mighty Men** offers a profound lesson for contemporary believers. Just as these warriors, filled with unwavering devotion and commitment, faced giants without fear, believers today must stand together, undeterred by challenges, united in their faith and commitment to **Christ**. The battle might have shifted from the physical realm to the spiritual, but the essence remains: to stand firm, be strong in faith, and remain devoted to the divine destiny of **Christ**.

David and His Mighty Men: A Symbol of Spiritual Warfare and Corporate Responsibility for the Lord's Throne

I. Introduction

The biblical account of David and his **Mighty Men** in the books of Samuel and Chronicles paints a vivid picture of courage, loyalty, and unwavering faith in the face of seemingly insurmountable challenges. Their stories serve not only as a historical recounting but also as a spiritual analogy for the Church's role in the cosmic battle between good and evil.

II. Corporate Responsibility for Throne Interests

David, the shepherd boy who rose to become the King of Israel, often found himself in situations where he was under threat from his enemies. A striking instance is found in the narrative where David was targeted by one of the giants, a descendant of the very Goliath whom David had defeated. In his peril, one of his **Mighty Men** came to his aid, saving him from imminent danger (2 Samuel 21:15-17, KJV). This intervention prompted David's men to advise him, **"Thou shalt go no more out with us to battle, that thou quench not the light of**

Israel" (2 Samuel 21:17, KJV).

This protective stance can be likened to the Church's responsibility to uphold and defend the honor, glory, and throne of **Jesus Christ**. Just as David's destiny was intertwined with his **Mighty Men**, the destiny of **Christ** and **His** Church are inextricably linked. Paul reminds us of this in Ephesians, **"And hath put all things under his feet, and gave him to be the head over all things to the church, which is his body, the fulness of him that filleth all in all" (Ephesians 1:22-23, KJV).** The warfare that believers engage in is not just a personal endeavor; it is a collective battle for the **Lord**'s sovereignty.

III. Suffering for The Body's Sake

The concept of vicarious suffering, or enduring hardship on behalf of others, is evident in the acts of David's **Mighty Men**. Their courage and valor served not only their own interests but also the broader interests of the nation of Israel. This mirrors Paul's ministry, who declared that he endured trials and sufferings **"for his body's sake, which is the church" (Colossians 1:24, KJV).**

Paul's sufferings weren't for his sins or personal shortcomings; **Christ** had already paid the ultimate price for those. Instead, Paul's struggles were aimed at advancing the Church's spiritual victory. **He** embodies the kind of spiritual strength and courage that believers ought to aspire to – the kind exemplified by David's **Mighty Men**. It's a reminder that true spiritual warfare requires believers to look beyond personal blessings and instead focus on the corporate well-being of the Church.

IV. A reminder of what God can do

David and his **Mighty Men** serve as a poignant reminder of the role's believers play in the grand narrative of **God's** redemptive plan. They symbolize the Church's call to defend the **Lord**'s honor and fight against spiritual forces. The stories underscore the need for believers to transition from a mindset of personal blessings to one of corporate responsibility, ensuring the advancement and victory of the Church. As we face our own "giants" in the spiritual realm, may we draw inspiration from these **Mighty Men**, remembering that our battles are not just personal skirmishes but are part of the larger war for the **Lord**'s Kingdom.

Mighty Men of God: A Biblical Analysis of Valor, Faith, and Leadership

The Bible is replete with tales of valor, faith, and leadership, often showcased by the **Mighty Men** who rose in times of crisis, trial, and triumph. These men exhibited characteristics that were both of this world—strength, skill, and courage—and of the spirit—faith, integrity, and devotion. Using the Bible, this teaching aims to elucidate 30 points of what it means to be a **Mighty** man of **God**, supported by scriptural examples.

#1. Faithfulness to God:

Scripture: "But thou, O man of **God**, flee these things; and follow after righteousness, **Godliness**, faith, love, patience, meekness." - 1 Timothy 6:11

#2. Courage in the Face of Adversity:
David facing Goliath is a testament to this.
Scripture: **"Then said David to the Philistine, Thou comest to me with a sword, and with a spear, and with a shield: but I come to thee in the name of the Lord of hosts, the God of the armies of Israel, whom thou hast defied." - 1 Samuel 17:45**

#3. Integrity and Righteousness:
Joseph resisting Potipar's wife is an example.
Scripture: **"And it came to pass after these things, that his master's wife cast her eyes upon Joseph; and she said, Lie with me. But he refused." - Genesis 39:7-8a**

#4. Leadership and Guidance:
Moses led the Israelites through the wilderness.
Scripture: **"And Moses said unto the Lord, O my Lord, I am not eloquent... but send, I pray thee, by the hand of him whom thou wilt send." - Exodus 4:10, 13b**

#5. Sacrificial Love:
Jonathan's love for David.
Scripture: **"And Jonathan caused David to swear again, because he loved him: for he loved him as he loved his own soul." - 1 Samuel 20:17**

#6. Willingness to Repent:
King David after his sin with Bathsheba.

Scripture: **"Create in me a clean heart, O God; and renew a right spirit within me." - Psalm 51:10**

#7. Standing Firm in Convictions:
Daniel in the lion's den.
Scripture: **"Now when Daniel knew that the writing was signed, he went into his house; and his windows being open in his chamber toward Jerusalem, he kneeled upon his knees three times a day, and prayed, and gave thanks before his God, as he did aforetime." - Daniel 6:10**

#8. Seeking God's Wisdom:
King Solomon's request for wisdom.
Scripture: **"And Solomon said, Thou hast shewed unto thy servant David my father great mercy, according as he walked before thee in truth, and in righteousness, and in uprightness of heart with thee; and thou hast kept for him this great kindness, that thou hast given him a son to sit on his throne, as it is this day." - 1 Kings 3:6**

#9. Being a Voice for the Voiceless:
Moses speaking up for the Israelites in Egypt.
Scripture: **"And Moses spake before the Lord, saying, Behold, the children of Israel have not hearkened unto me; how then shall Pharaoh hear me, who am of uncircumcised lips?" - Exodus 6:12**

#10. Trust in God's Plan:
Abraham's willingness to sacrifice Isaac.
Scripture: **"And Abraham said, My son, God will provide himself a lamb for a burnt offering: so they**

went both of them together." - Genesis 22:8

Mighty Men in the Bible:

The Bible chronicles the lives of many **Mighty Men** such as Joshua, who led the Israelites into the Promised Land; Samson, who was granted supernatural strength; and the Apostle Paul, who spread the gospel to the Gentiles. Each of these men exhibited the characteristics mentioned above, displaying both their physical and spiritual prowess in the service of **God**.

The Bible's portrayal of **Mighty Men** serves as an inspiration and a guide for believers today. To be a **Mighty** man of **God** is not solely about physical strength or prowess but more about spiritual strength, integrity, faith, and a deep relationship with **God**. These accounts beckon every believer to rise, take up their cross, and march forth in faith, exemplifying the might of **God** in every action and decision.

The Power of Faith in the Face of Adversity

As we delve deep into the scriptures, let us turn our Bibles to 1 Samuel 17. We embarking on a journey of understanding the multifaceted nature of faith. Contrary to the common belief that there's just one or perhaps two to three ways faith comes to us, scripture reveals at least 28 ways, as Pastor Mike has expounded upon in a book available on Amazon.

Why this emphasis on faith, one may ask? Simply put, faith is essential. The lifeblood of a Christian's relationship with **God**. When **Christ** proclaimed, **"Thy faith hath made thee whole," (Mark 10:52 KJV), He** was essentially emphasizing the immense power of trust in **Him. He** sought to highlight that one's unwavering confidence, reliance, and dependence on Him was the path to spiritual wholeness.

Before the fall of man, the Garden of Eden was a sanctuary where man existed in complete harmony and faith with **God**. For, **"Through faith we understand that the worlds were framed by the word of God, so that things which are seen were not made of things which do appear." (Hebrews 11:3 KJV).** This scripture delineates that faith, a spiritual substance, is foundational to creation and existence.

It's crucial to grasp the enormity of faith's significance. Faith outside of **Christ**, stripped of its spiritual gravity, is rendered as mere vain imagination, lacking substance and verity. The kind of faith that the Bible underscores, the faith that truly counts, is unwavering trust in **God**. In the celebrated chapter of Hebrews 11, we are presented with a pantheon of heroes, champions, if you will, who were true paragons of faith.

Within the lush landscapes of the Garden of Eden stood two trees of great import - The Tree of Life and the Tree of Knowledge of Good and Evil. While interpretations vary, one might posit that the former represents unwavering faith in **God's** word and decrees, while the latter epitomizes the perils of doubt and unbelief. It was this very act of succumbing to doubt and partaking of the forbidden fruit that cast humanity into a state of spiritual depravity, transporting them from a realm of unwavering faith to one dominated by unbelief and fleshly desires. The scripture exhorts believers with the words, **"[This] I say then, Walk in the Spirit, and ye shall not fulfil the lust of the flesh." (Galatians 5:16 KJV).**

This dichotomy between faith and unbelief underscores the eternal struggle of man. Yet, as believers, it's imperative to recognize our inherent design – we are beings sculpted in the image of faith. The metaphor of **Christ** being the vine and believers the branches highlights this interconnectedness, emphasizing the necessity of faith. For **"For by grace are ye saved through faith; and that not of yourselves: it is the gift of God:" (Ephesians 2:8 KJV).** All aspects of spiritual sustenance, be it wisdom, hope, righteousness, or obedience, are mediated through faith.

In , while the world may constantly vacillate between belief and doubt, as followers of **Christ**, we are called to anchor ourselves in the unshakeable faith of our Savior. In doing so, not only do we honor **His** sacrifice, but we also pave the way for a spiritual journey filled with divine revelations, blessings, and the true fulfillment of **God's** purpose for our lives.

Walking in Faith and Trusting the Unseen

"Now faith is the substance of things hoped for, the

evidence of things not seen." - Hebrews 11:1 (KJV)

In a world inundated by sensory perceptions, it's easy to fall victim to unbelief. We are continually prompted by what we see, feel, hear, and smell. But it is essential to recognize the detrimental voice of the devil - the voice of unbelief that murmurs: "**God** doesn't love you. **God** won't forgive you. **God** doesn't care." Yet, amidst these voices, there stands an unwavering truth: the voice of the Father, the Son, and the Holy Ghost, affirming us, "trust me. Believe me. Depend upon me."

"The thief cometh not, but for to steal, and to kill, and to destroy: I am come that they might have life, and that they might have it more abundantly." - John 10:10 (KJV)

Every child is born with an innate sense of faith. The Bible says, "Verily I say unto you, Except ye be converted, and become as little children, ye shall not enter into the kingdom of heaven." - Matthew 18:3 (KJV). This childlike faith, however, is vulnerable. As children grow, deceit and disappointments often erode this faith. But **Jesus** came to restore our faith, not in man, but in **Him.**

Man will fail us, as scripture attests, **"Thus saith the LORD; Cursed be the man that trusteth in man, and maketh flesh his arm, and whose heart departeth from the LORD." - Jeremiah 17:5 (KJV).** But **Jesus Christ** is the bedrock of our hope. In **Him,** as we walk in faith, all things become possible.

"**Jesus** said unto him, **If thou canst believe, all things are possible to him that believeth." - Mark 9:23 (KJV)**

As we delve into 1 Samuel 17, we see a clear manifestation of faith in action. Just as the physical body can be trained and strengthened through various exercises, so can our spiritual faith muscle be developed. The Apostle Paul reminds us, **"For bodily exercise profiteth little: but Godliness is profitable unto all things, having promise of the life that now is, and of that which is to come." - 1 Timothy 4:8 (KJV).**

In the journey of faith, there are challenges and obstacles. However, testimonies of healing, provision, and miraculous interventions demonstrate the power of unwavering faith. The journey may be riddled with the school of hard knocks, but in **Christ**, victory is assured.

In , faith is not just a passive acknowledgment but an active trust in **God's** ability, even when circumstances seem contrary. It is the substance of our hope and the evidence of the unseen. To truly live victorious lives as **God's Mighty Men**, we must continually nurture and build our faith, trusting wholly in **Christ**.

"But without faith it is impossible to please him: for he that cometh to God must believe that he is, and that he is a rewarder of them that diligently seek him." - Hebrews 11:6 (KJV)

CHAPTER TWO

"God's Mighty Men: Standing Firm in Tempestuous Times"

In the book of Ephesians, we read, **"Wherefore take unto you the whole armour of God, that ye may be able to withstand in the evil day, and having done all, to stand" (Ephesians 6:13, KJV).** These times that we live in can aptly be described as "evil days" – times of peril and uncertainty where faith is tried and tested. The state of the world today reminds us of the importance of building our lives on the unshakeable foundation of **God's** Word. **Jesus** himself warned, **"And every one that heareth these sayings of mine, and doeth them not, shall be likened unto a foolish man, which built his house upon the sand: And the rain descended, and the floods came, and the winds blew, and beat upon that house; and it fell: and great was the fall of it" (Matthew 7:26-27, KJV).**

We are witnessing a time of increasing exposure, where true characters are revealed, and the genuineness of our faith is being refined. Pastors and spiritual leaders are not immune. Every believer, regardless of their position, is called to a life of repentance and alignment with **God's** Word. David's heartfelt prayer resonates deeply, **"Search me, O God, and know my heart: try me, and know my**

thoughts: And see if there be any wicked way in me, and lead me in the way everlasting" (Psalm 139:23-24, KJV).

One powerful method to remain aligned with **God** is to meditate upon **His** Word and establish a personal relationship with **Him.** The Psalmist declares, **"Thy word have I hid in mine heart, that I might not sin against thee" (Psalm 119:11, KJV).** By hiding **God's** Word in our heart, we not only equip ourselves against sin but also fine-tune our spiritual ears to hear **His** voice clearly amidst the cacophony of life. The Bible is a guiding light, and every believer should embrace its teachings and apply them in every aspect of life, including relationships.

The relationships we foster, especially marital bonds, are a testament to our walk with **God**. The Apostle Paul wrote to the Ephesians about husbands, **"Husbands, love your wives, even as Christ also loved the church, and gave himself for it" (Ephesians 5:25, KJV).** When we fail to mirror **Christ**'s sacrificial love in our marriages, we give the adversary an opening. As believers, we must remember the sanctity of these covenants and uphold them with love, respect, and dedication. When confronted with challenges in our relationships, turning to **God's** Word provides guidance and wisdom. **Proverbs 3:5-6** tells us, **"Trust in the LORD with all thine heart; and lean not unto thine own understanding. In all thy ways acknowledge him, and he shall direct thy paths" (KJV).**

In, as **God's Mighty Men** and women, it is imperative to stand firm in our faith, especially in tempestuous times. By deeply rooting ourselves in the Word of **God**, we can withstand the storms of life. And by applying biblical principles to our relationships, we not only strengthen our bonds with our loved ones but also showcase **Christ**'s love to the world. Let us remain vigilant, steadfast in our faith, and let the Word of **God** be our guiding light in all that we do.

Overcoming in the Realm of Faith

"I press toward the mark for the prize of the high calling of God in Christ Jesus." - Philippians 3:14 (KJV)

In the tapestry of our spiritual walk, there's a paramount truth: that our journey is one of unwavering faith, a testament to **God's** power within us, and a commitment to push forward, irrespective of past failures or barriers. Paul, in his epistle to the Philippians, proclaims that he hasn't fully reached the apex of his spiritual destiny. Yet, he remains undeterred, **"forgetting those things which are behind and reaching forth unto those things which are before..." (Philippians 3:13, KJV).** This isn't about past achievements or accolades; it's a humble assertion of a continuous journey towards **Christ**'s high calling.

The hope we find in **Christ Jesus** is unparalleled. Our living **God** is not a mere deity from ancient tales but one who has defeated death and made **His** abode within us. **"He is not here: for he is risen, as he said. Come, see the place where the Lord lay." (Matthew 28:6, KJV).** Such overwhelming truth should stir our souls, ignite a joy that cannot be contained, and drive us to a worship that's unbridled and uninhibited.

Often, we question **God's** plan, especially when it seems we've been placed in spiritually barren territories. These 'dead zones', as some might call them, may seem devoid of fervor, passion, or genuine worship. Yet could it be that **God** intentionally plants us in these areas to bring a spiritual revival? The scripture reminds us, **"The dead praise not the Lord, neither any that go down into silence." (Psalm 115:17, KJV).** But here's the revelation: If you're alive in **Christ**, then you're called to break that silence and bring the dead regions to life!

When we dive into the narrative of 1 Samuel 17, the Philistines present a formidable challenge to the Israelites. Their champion, Goliath of Gath, stood as a giant, both in stature and intimidation. The scripture describes him, saying, **"And there went out a champion out of the camp of the Philistines, named Goliath, of Gath, whose height was six cubits and a span." (1 Samuel 17:4, KJV).** However, it is crucial not to be ensnared by the grandeur of challenges but to focus on the grandness of **God's** might and the men **He** empowers.

In , God's Mighty Men are those who, irrespective of circumstances, challenges, or environments, choose to press forward in faith. They are the Davids in a world of

Goliaths, the voices in spiritually silent zones, and the bearers of **Christ**'s resurrection power. To be **God's Mighty** man or woman is to live in unwavering faith, always pressing towards the mark set by **Christ Jesus**. Let us rise, awaken the dormant, and be the conduits of revival in every sphere we occupy! Amen.

A Call to Authentic Worship and Faith

The scriptures are replete with messages that urge us to exalt only the **Lord** our **God**, as we are vividly reminded in **Exodus 20:3, "Thou shalt have no other Gods before me."** Worship, a term deeply rooted in biblical tradition, signifies an intense reverence, adoration, and homage rendered to **God**. In essence, it means to humbly bow down and kiss the feet of the Almighty or to sing praises exalting **His** glory.

Yet, contemporary Christianity finds itself amid a quagmire of misplaced adoration. In place of the pure, undiluted worship of **God**, there's been a subtle shift towards idolatry. This idolatry isn't always towards physical idols but towards intangible things such as personal problems, financial difficulties, sicknesses, or even external societal issues. When **Jesus** proclaimed, **"Thou shalt worship the Lord thy God, and him only shalt thou serve" (Matthew 4:10 KJV), He** was emphasizing the exclusive devotion one should have for **God** alone.

An apt reflection of this misplaced reverence can be seen

in the account of David and Goliath. The Israelites were not only filled with fear but were also continuously talking about the Philistine giant, essentially giving him more reverence than he deserved. They were exalting him instead of putting their faith in the might of the **Lord**. This narrative from 1 Samuel 17 reminds us that what we exalt or give importance to ultimately occupies our heart.

It is imperative for us to recognize this drift. For if we exalt unbelief, our hearts will undoubtedly be filled with doubts. The scripture reassures in **Hebrews 11:1, "Now faith is the substance of things hoped for, the evidence of things not seen."** We must remember that the same **God** who calls us to have faith is also the one who took away our sins and infirmities.

Jesus, throughout **His** ministry, showcased the importance of surrounding oneself with faith. There were instances when **He** would only pray in the presence of those who genuinely believed in **His** power. **He** sought the company of those who trusted in **God's** might. This highlights the fact that in our battles too, it is crucial to be surrounded by people who possess unwavering faith, for their faith can uplift us.

Past experiences have shown that unbelief can lead one astray, making one forget even the foundational scriptures. However, by constantly immersing ourselves in **God's** Word and prayer, we can navigate back to the path of faith. As it is beautifully expressed in **Romans 10:17, "So then faith cometh by hearing, and hearing by the word of God."**

In , being **God's Mighty Men** and women calls for a resolute faith that refuses to exalt anything above **God**. It demands an unshakable belief that recognizes ailments, not as personal possessions but as the enemy's deception. It beckons us to step into the identity that **God** has conferred upon us, an identity rooted in faith, hope, and worship. As believers, let our worship be pure, our faith unwavering, and our praises be unto the **Lord** alone.

Rise Up: God's Mighty Men in the Realm of Faith

"Yea, though I walk through the valley of the shadow of death, I will fear no evil: for thou art with me; thy rod and thy staff they comfort me." - Psalm 23:4 (KJV)

Throughout history, we've witnessed the rise and fall of champions. The Philistines had their champion in Goliath. A giant so formidable that the Israelites saw him as a **God**, causing them to tremble in fear. But it was written, **"And when Saul and all Israel heard those words of the Philistine, they were dismayed, and greatly afraid." - 1 Samuel 17:11 (KJV).** Goliath's presence brought a test of faith.

Yet, amidst the ranks of the fearful was David, a man after **God's** own heart. A young shepherd boy, anointed to be king, and a testament to the power of faith. "Rise Up," we are beckoned. Rise up as **Mighty Men** and women of faith. For are we not more than conquerors?

"Nay, in all these things we are more than conquerors through him that loved us." - Romans 8:37 (KJV).

In the face of adversities, challenges, and doubts, our anchor must remain in the **Lord**. **"Greater is he that is in you, than he that is in the world." - 1 John 4:4 (KJV).** We have been reminded time and time again, **"If God be for us, who can be against us?" - Romans 8:31 (KJV).**

Our source of strength is Christ. As it's penned, "No weapon that is formed against thee shall prosper; and every tongue that shall rise against thee in judgment thou shalt condemn." - Isaiah 54:17 (KJV). However, the key to harnessing this strength lies in our connection to **Him.** As **Christ** himself said, **"I am the vine, ye are the branches: He that abideth in me, and I in him, the same bringeth forth much fruit: for without me ye can do nothing." - John 15:5 (KJV).**

It's the Word that nourishes and sustains us. **"In the beginning was the Word, and the Word was with God, and the Word was God." - John 1:1 (KJV)**. Our faith is fueled by our immersion in the Scriptures and our commitment to walking the path of righteousness.

David's strength wasn't drawn from his physical prowess or his position but from his unwavering faith in **God**. **He** was a worshiper. And through worship, faith blossoms. For faith comes by hearing and hearing by the Word of **God**. David's heart sang praises to the **Lord**, nurturing a faith so robust that he could face giants without fear.

However, even in our journey, we must be cautious of where we place our focus. The world presents many champions, but not all champion the cause of **Christ**. Our champion is the epitome of righteousness, holiness, and obedience.

Living in the realm of faith requires unwavering commitment and dedication to the Word of **God**. It requires making **Christ** the center of our lives and building a personal relationship with **Him.** David's faith wasn't passive; it was active, thriving, and bold. Like David, we are called to rise up as **God's Mighty Men** and women, confronting our giants with faith and drawing strength from the promises of **God**. For in faith, we find victory.

The Wonders of God's Mighty Men: Faith and Protection in the Midst of Fire

The strength of the human spirit, combined with the grace and protection of **God**, has been showcased in the scriptures and through countless testimonies over time. The biblical stories about **God's Mighty Men** are not just limited to historical records but are being lived and experienced even today. The Bible is replete with instances where faith led to divine intervention, protection, and miracles.

The Power of Faith in Christ in Moments of Danger
One such testimony is when I found my self engulfed in

the flames of a gasoline fire. But the same fire that consumes, through **God's** grace, transformed into a testament of **God**s protective shield. Such an experience evokes memories of Shadrach, Meshach, and Abednego, three of **God's** faithful servants who were thrown into a blazing furnace yet emerged without even the smell of smoke on them.

"And these three men, Shadrach, Meshach, and Abednego, fell down bound into the midst of the burning fiery furnace. Then Nebuchadnezzar the king was astounded, and rose up in haste, and spake, and said unto his counsellors, Did not we cast three men bound into the midst of the fire? They answered and said unto the king, True, O king. He answered and said, Lo, I see four men loose, walking in the midst of the fire, and they have no hurt; and the form of the fourth is like the Son of God." (Daniel 3:23-25 KJV).

The Shield of Protection for Those Who Act in Faith

Another incident narrates the unthinking, instinctual act of picking up a blazing hot skillet, a moment that should have caused severe injury. Yet, by divine intervention, only a mild pinkness was seen, reminiscent of **God's** protective hand on **His** faithful servants. The Bible frequently alludes to the protection of those who have faith:

"But the Lord is faithful, who shall stablish you, and keep you from evil." (2 Thessalonians 3:3 KJV).

Faith as a Catalyst for Wonders

These events underline a crucial point: being full of faith turns ordinary men into signs and wonders. To the onlooker, these events seem miraculous, something beyond human comprehension. Yet, to the believer, it's a testament to the power of faith and **God's** promise to protect and favor those who trust in **Him.**

"For we walk by faith, not by sight." (2 Corinthians 5:7 KJV).

Divine Provision in Financial Challenges

Churches and believers often find themselves in situations where their needs surpass their apparent resources. Yet, through faith and dependence on **God**, these financial challenges are met, showcasing **God's** continuous providence. The Bible assures believers of **God's** provision:

"But my God shall supply all your need according to his riches in glory by Christ Jesus." (Philippians 4:19 KJV).

Standing Firm in Faith Amidst Challenges

Challenges, whether they come in the form of criticisms or attempts to change one's stand on **God's** word, are not new. Yet, staying true to **God's** message and not compromising for worldly gains is what sets **God's Mighty Men** apart. Paul, an apostle of **Christ**, encountered numerous such challenges and exhorted believers:

"Watch ye, stand fast in the faith, quit you like men, be strong." (1 Corinthians 16:13 KJV).

The stories of **God's Mighty Men** are not tales of the past; they continue to unfold even today. They remind us that when we are filled with faith, walk in **His** ways, and rely on **Him, God** shows up. **He** shields, protects, provides, and establishes **His** children as signs and wonders. In moments of peril, uncertainty, or challenge, **God's** word stands true, and **His** promises remain unbroken. Through faith, believers become living testimonies of **His** might, making them indeed, **God's Mighty Men**.

God's Mighty Men: The Power of Faith in Action

"Ye are of God, little children, and have overcome them: because greater is he that is in you, than he that is in the world." - 1 John 4:4 (KJV)

Throughout the Scriptures, we find tales of individuals who refused to be daunted by life's gargantuan challenges. In our current narrative, David's story from the biblical account emerges as a paragon of faith amidst adversity. When the **Mighty** Goliath taunted Israel, it wasn't the size or might of the giant that mattered; it was the size of the **God** whom David served. David confidently said, **"The LORD that delivered me out of the paw of the lion, and out of the paw of the bear, he will deliver me out of the hand of this Philistine." - 1 Samuel 17:37 (KJV)**

Many a time, we unintentionally elevate our problems, just like how some Israelites might have exaggerated Goliath's prowess. However, David never saw Goliath as a giant. Instead, he saw an uncircumcised Philistine challenging the armies of the living **God**. David's viewpoint was clear: **"Who is this uncircumcised Philistine, that he should defy the armies of the living God?" - 1 Samuel 17:26 (KJV)**

Often, our utterances reflect our spiritual position. When words of doubt escape our lips, it acts as a barometer, indicating our waning faith. **"So then faith cometh by hearing, and hearing by the word of God." - Romans 10:17 (KJV)** To combat this, it's imperative to hide **God's** Word in our hearts, letting it serve as our guiding light.

Experiences shared here resonate with the biblical exhortation: **"For we walk by faith, not by sight." - 2 Corinthians 5:7 (KJV).** Healing, deliverance, and miraculous encounters aren't pursued; they follow those who ardently believe. Every adversity faced is an opportunity to display resolute faith. While infirmities and ailments may be factual, the truth remains: **"But he was wounded for our transgressions, he was bruised for our iniquities: the chastisement of our peace was upon him; and with his stripes we are healed." - Isaiah 53:5 (KJV)**

Just as I have reclaimed my health and sensory experiences by taking a bold stance in faith, you too can experience breakthroughs by confronting every challenge with the knowledge that **Jesus** has already paid the price.

In , God's Mighty Men aren't defined by their physical prowess, but by their unwavering faith in **Him.** David was not a warrior by profession, but his unwavering trust in **God** and understanding of divine promises allowed him to defeat what many perceived as an insurmountable foe. As believers today, our challenges may differ, but the principles remain. By grounding ourselves in the Word and rising up in faith, we can overcome the Goliaths in our lives, not by our might, but by the Spirit of the **Lord**. **"Not by might, nor by power, but by my spirit, saith the LORD of hosts." - Zechariah 4:6 (KJV).**

A Discourse on Faith and Victory

In our walk of faith, there are moments that challenge our beliefs and our steadfastness. It is during these moments that we discover our true selves and where our allegiance lies. The story of David, as depicted in the Bible, provides a compelling example of unwavering faith, courage, and victory against all odds.

One of the fascinating aspects of our faith is the personal relationship we develop with **God**. There are instances in our lives where we talk to our ailments, our fears, and our weaknesses. Just as I spoke to my lungs and experienced healing, you too can experience the transformative power of faith. **"And all things, whatsoever ye shall ask in prayer, believing, ye shall receive." – Matthew 21:22**

(KJV)

In recounting experiences, I have faced situations that could have easily triggered past fears and ailments. Yet, the overpowering presence of **God** prevailed. Much like David, who faced the giant Goliath and said, **"Who is this uncircumcised Philistine, that he should defy the armies of the living God?" – 1 Samuel 17:26 (KJV).** The mention of "uncircumcised" emphasizes the lack of a covenant with **God**, showcasing David's unwavering faith in the divine covenant he held.

Often, the world around us may seem like it's celebrating wickedness, but as believers, we must keep our eyes fixed on **Jesus**. We are reminded, **"And I, if I be lifted up from the earth, will draw all men unto me." – John 12:32 (KJV).** We should continually exalt and praise **Jesus**, our ultimate champion, who epitomizes purity, righteousness, and holiness.

It's important to acknowledge our human nature. Yes, we falter and sin. **"If we say that we have no sin, we deceive ourselves, and the truth is not in us." – 1 John 1:8 (KJV).** However, it's also paramount to recognize the victories over sin and adversities. Through **God's** grace, as mentioned in Galatians, we overcome. **"Now the works of the flesh are manifest, which are these; Adultery, fornication, uncleanness, lasciviousness... and such like: of the which I tell you before, as I have also told you in time past, that they which do such things shall not inherit the kingdom of God." – Galatians 5:19-21 (KJV).**

David's encounter with Goliath teaches us not to be swayed by unbelief or to respond with negativity. David, instead of lashing out at the unbelieving soldiers, took the challenge with faith. The spirit of faith is characterized by kindness, gentleness, meekness, long-suffering, and forgiveness. When we encounter others struggling with their faith, it's our duty to uplift, inspire, and remind them of the omnipotent presence within them, **"Ye are of God, little children, and have overcome them: because greater is he that is in you, than he that is in the world." – 1 John 4:4 (KJV).**

The tales of **Mighty Men** of **God**, such as David, are not just ancient stories but real-life applications for us. They challenge us to embrace our faith, face our Goliaths, and stand unwavering in the face of adversities. Our journey, filled with both trials and victories, is a testament to the unfathomable power of belief and the **Mighty** presence of **God** in our lives. Let us take heart and be of good cheer, for in **Him,** we are more than conquerors.

Faith Through Trials and Association

In our spiritual journey, we often find ourselves in a struggle between faith and doubt. The Bible beautifully encapsulates the essence of this struggle through its various characters, demonstrating the power of association and unwavering belief in the face of adversity.

Another avenue through which faith is strengthened is by

association. As the scriptures highlight, the company we keep can greatly influence our spirit. In the book of Numbers, we read about Joshua and Caleb, two men who were distinctly different from their peers. The majority brought back a negative report about the Promised Land, but Joshua and Caleb had a spirit of faith.

"But my servant Caleb, because he had another spirit with him, and hath followed me fully, him will I bring into the land whereinto he went; and his seed shall possess it." (Numbers 14:24 KJV)

Association with those who possess a spirit of faith, like Joshua and Caleb, is pivotal. On the other hand, it's equally crucial to discern and distance oneself from those who preach unbelief and misconstrued grace. True grace isn't a license to sin; rather, it's a divine empowerment to overcome sin.

"For the grace of God that bringeth salvation hath appeared to all men, Teaching us that, denying unGodliness and worldly lusts, we should live soberly, righteously, and Godly, in this present world;" (Titus 2:11-12 KJV)

It's not about self-righteousness or boasting in our works, but it's about exalting the one who resides within us. The Apostle Paul reminds us:

"But God forbid that I should glory, save in the cross of our Lord Jesus Christ, by whom the world is crucified unto me, and I unto the world." (Galatians 6:14 KJV)

In times of adversity, the true nature of our faith is revealed. We're reminded of David, who faced criticism from his own family, yet his faith remained unshaken. Similarly, the spirit of faith isn't about arrogance or superiority; it's about humility and recognizing the grace of **God** in our lives.

"With all lowliness and meekness, with longsuffering, forbearing one another in love;" (Ephesians 4:2 KJV)

In moments of desperation, when our faith seems to waver, crying out for mercy can open the floodgates of **God's** grace. The story of my son being healed from rabies is a testament to the power of persistent prayer, crying out for mercy, for sixteen hours, with unwavering faith in **God's** ability to perform miracles.

In, our journey of faith is strewn with challenges and adversities, but it's through these very experiences that our faith grows. Whether it's by the company we keep or the battles we face, our trust in **God** deepens. The stories of **God's Mighty Men**, like Joshua, Caleb, David, and many others, serve as reminders of the indomitable spirit of faith that we are called to embody. Through trials, through associations, and through fervent prayers, may our faith remain unshaken, rooted deeply in the love and grace of our **Lord**. Hallelujah!

Unyielding Faith in the Face of Adversity

"But without faith it is impossible to please him: for he that cometh to God must believe that he is, and that he is a rewarder of them that diligently seek him." - Hebrews 11:6 (KJV)

Undoubtedly, our world is marred by challenges, temptations, and despair. In these trying times, humanity often cries out for mercy. This plea resonates with the biblical narratives wherein blind Bartimaeus cried, **"Have mercy on me" (Mark 10:47 KJV),** the ten lepers begged, **"Jesus, Master, have mercy on us!" (Luke 17:13 KJV),** and the Canaanite woman implored, **"Lord, have mercy on me" (Matthew 15:22 KJV).** These desperate cries demonstrate an unwavering faith in the **Lord**'s mercy.

God's mercy is an immense comfort. It is an assurance that though we may face storms, **His** grace remains unwavering. But to access this mercy, one must have faith. A faith that can turn a dire situation into a testament of **God's** unending love.

God's presence in the church serves as a testament to **His** mercy and love. It seeks to ignite passion within the followers of **Christ**, not to engage in worldly conflicts or criticize the fallen. For, **"Judge not, that ye be not judged" (Matthew 7:1 KJV)**. Instead, it emphasizes the importance of addressing the spirit of unbelief. As faith diminishes, immorality and wickedness rise. But when the church becomes a beacon of faith and shows the true nature of **Christ**, the spirit of faith gets rekindled in many hearts.

Jesus serves as the epitome of faith, stating, **"The Spirit of the Lord is upon me" (Luke 4:18 KJV). His** unwavering trust in the Father is a testament that only through faith can one be filled with the Holy Spirit.

Faith is nourished by testimonials of **God's** power and mercy. Narratives of miraculous interventions, like the ones mentioned in the book "Living in Around with Miraculous", reveal **God's** power in everyday lives. On the other hand, tales of personal mistakes, such as those in "I Need **God** because I'm Stupid", underscore **God's** immense mercy even when we falter.

The ultimate challenge for believers is to stay focused on **Jesus**. David's encounter with his brother is a poignant reminder. When confronted, David exclaimed, **"Is there not a cause?" (1 Samuel 17:29 KJV).** David did not waste his time defending his faith to his brother. Instead, he chose to trust in **God**. Similarly, individuals full of faith might not fit into the worldly molds. Their unyielding trust in **God** makes them stand apart.

"What shall we then say to these things? If God be for us, who can be against us?" - Romans 8:31 (KJV)

In the panorama of human experience, challenges are inevitable. Yet, with faith in **God's** mercy and love, believers can overcome these adversities. This teaching serves as a testament to the power of faith in the **Lord**'s mercy. Just as blind Bartimaeus, the ten lepers, and the Canaanite woman cried out to **Jesus** and were shown mercy, believers today can also experience the transformative power of **God's** grace. To access this divine mercy, one must have unwavering faith, remain focused on **Jesus**, and be a beacon of hope and love in a world filled with despair.

The Perils of Misplaced Worship

Misplaced worship is not a new phenomenon. As we trace back to the early Biblical days, Israel was engrossed in idolatry, constructing altars on every hill and beneath every tree. This act can be likened to the modern-day church, where idolatry has seemingly taken on a new form.

"Why is the church so lukewarm, lackadaisical, and non-committed, both in America and across the globe?" One might ask. The answer lies in the current objects of their adoration: vain amusements, personal problems, perpetual anxiety, and the never-ending quest for either financial abundance or the lament of its lack. Rather than directing their attention towards **Jesus Christ**, many are preoccupied with political happenings and daily distractions.

The Apostle Paul emphatically stated, **"Preach the Word, instant in season and out of season."** Yet, contrary to his counsel, numerous contemporary preachers choose to propagate their personal desires and narratives. The departure from authentic scriptures has a notable consequence: without the unwavering Word of **God** as the foundation, the Holy Spirit cannot affirm **His** message.

"Philippians 4:8 - Finally, brethren, whatsoever things are true, whatsoever things are honest, whatsoever things are just, whatsoever things are pure, whatsoever things are lovely, whatsoever things are of good report; if there be any virtue, and if there be any praise, think on these things."

Acting on the Word of **God** is paramount, for mere hearing without implementation leads to self-deception. An encounter with **God** highlighted this for me. In an intimate moment of prayer, **God** articulated a profound revelation to me. **He** said: **"Stop Worshipping The Devil!"** I was initially stunned. Yet, **His** clarifications were clear: desist from lamenting physical symptoms, cease the complaints of financial shortcomings, and abstain from the glorification of government actions, politics, or the missteps of the wayward church. In essence, give the adversary no acknowledgment.

For isn't He, our Lord, superior to these worldly concerns?

The book of Revelation illuminates the essence of worship. It describes the adoration of **God** approximately 8 to 10 times. Intriguingly, it also mentions worship of the beast, the antichrist, and the devil with almost equal frequency. Such emphasis on worship is pivotal because adoring **Christ** cultivates faith, while exalting the devil breeds doubt.

"James 1:8 - A double minded man is unstable in all

his ways." The devil, bound for eternal damnation, craves adulation. As for me, my heart seeks to overflow with faith; thus, I will venerate none other than **God**. The outcomes of our worship are clear: if one glorifies the devil, they become consumed with negative emotions like anger and fear. Conversely, if we overflow with praise and worship for **God** and **Jesus Christ**, we are infused with faith, love, joy, peace, and victory.

"Colossians 3:16 - Let the word of Christ dwell in you richly in all wisdom; teaching and admonishing one another in psalms and hymns and spiritual songs, singing with grace in your hearts to the Lord."

The direction of our worship shapes our spiritual trajectory. Let us be wary of unintentionally glorifying that which detracts from **God's** glory. In a world full of distractions, let's choose to magnify **God**, embodying faith and righteousness, and guarding against the perils of misplaced worship.

Warriors of Faith

"Give not that which is holy unto the dogs, neither cast ye your pearls before swine, lest they trample them under their feet, and turn again and rend you." (Matthew 7:6 KJV)

Throughout the ages, powerful men and women of **God**

have stood tall, unwavering in the face of challenges and difficulties. I, once had a board of elders that stood by him, supporting and upholding the work of the ministry. Yet, the winds of time and fate took many of them home, to be with the **Lord** in glory. The testimony of such dedicated souls underscores the need for true discipleship, commitment, and teaching.

"For what is a man profited, if he shall gain the whole world, and lose his own soul? or what shall a man give in exchange for his soul?" (Matthew 16:26 KJV)

It is easy to misconstrue earthly blessings as the sole determinants of divine favor. While the world may think that financial prosperity is the true sign of success, **Jesus** reminds us that true wealth is laid up in heaven. This is a divine salary, eternal and incorruptible. The treasures of heaven surpass any earthly measure.

The biblical account of David and King Saul is a powerful illustration of the distinction between man's perspective and **God's**. When David, a young lad, volunteered to fight the Philistine giant Goliath, King Saul was skeptical. However, David's retort was profound, recounting how, with **God's** strength, he had defeated both a lion and a bear to protect his sheep. This was not David's might, but **God's**.

"Thy adversary the devil, as a roaring lion, walketh about, seeking whom he may devour: whom resist stedfast in the faith, knowing that the same afflictions are accomplished in your brethren that are in the world." (1 Peter 5:8-9 KJV)

Life's challenges and temptations, both great and small, are incessant. However, letting even a small act of disobedience or compromise into our lives can give the devil an inroad. It is crucial to be vigilant, not yielding ground to the enemy. To live in victory, one must consistently resist the devil and remain steadfast in faith.

"Submit yourselves therefore to God. Resist the devil, and he will flee from you." (James 4:7 KJV)

Faith, in its true essence, does not waver based on circumstances. The Scriptures, from Genesis to Revelation, proclaim **God's** power, love, and willingness to heal and restore. **Jesus**, the same yesterday, today, and forever, healed all who came to Him in faith. It is this unwavering faith in the healing power of **God** that I have held onto, experiencing divine healing time and again.

"Fight the good fight of faith, lay hold on eternal life, whereunto thou art also called, and hast professed a good profession before many witnesses." (1 Timothy 6:12 KJV)

The journey of faith is not without its battles. It demands courage, persistence, and an unyielding trust in the power and promises of **God**. Like the **Mighty Men** and women of old, believers today are called to rise, resist the enemy, and lay hold of the victorious life in **Christ**. Rise up and fight!

The tales of **God's Mighty Men** echo through the corridors of time, reminding each generation of the power of faith, obedience, and dedication. These warriors, though faced with insurmountable odds, chose to stand firm, grounded in the truths of the Scriptures. May their testimonies inspire us to rise up, clad in the armor of **God**, ready to face the challenges of our day with unwavering faith.

The Spirit of Faith and the Power of the Word

In the annals of biblical history, there have been men of valor, men of faith who rose above their natural circumstances, clinging to the promises of **God** and the audacity of unwavering faith. Among these stalwarts stands David, an epitome of faith and courage, who rose from being a shepherd boy to the King of Israel.

"And David said to the Philistine, Thou comest to me with a sword, and with a spear, and with a shield: but I come to thee in the name of the LORD of hosts, the God of the armies of Israel, whom thou hast defied." - 1 Samuel 17:45 KJV

David, apart from his personal feats, was surrounded by 300 **Mighty Men**, warriors whose tales of valor reverberate through time. One such story speaks of a lentil field, a patch of land annually besieged by enemies. Every year, after months of hard work, just as the harvest was ripe, foes would come and strip away all that the men had toiled for. But one year, one man had had enough. Inspired by David's faith when he vanquished Goliath, this man resolved to stand his ground. No longer would he flee from his patch of land. **He** took a stand, embodying the very spirit of faith that David had shown against Goliath.

It is this spirit of faith that all believers are called to embrace. A faith that, in the face of adversity, instead of succumbing to fear, declares the promises of **God** with audacity.

A common misconception in today's world is that one must either rely solely on faith or solely on the physical remedies of this world, such as doctors and medicines. But the truth is more nuanced. Doctors have their place, and medicine can be a tool in the hands of the Great Physician. However, our ultimate trust should be in the **Lord**.

"He healeth the broken in heart, and bindeth up their wounds." - Psalm 147:3 KJV

My personal experience with arthritis serves as an illustrative testimony. While many may passively accept the ailment, blaming it on lineage or genetics, a true believer, grounded in the Word, can rise above. I chose to confront the affliction, using the authority vested in and through **Christ**. By declaring the Word of **God** over my situation and refusing to let my body dictate my actions, **God** supernaturally healed me over 30 years ago!

"Behold, I give unto you power to tread on serpents and scorpions, and over all the power of the enemy: and nothing shall by any means hurt you." - Luke 10:19 KJV

In a world teeming with challenges, be they giants of old or modern-day ailments, believers are called to a life of audacious faith. A faith that doesn't cower in the face of adversity but stands on the promises of **God**. David and his **Mighty Men** serve as timeless reminders that with **God** on our side, no giant is too big, no challenge insurmountable. As we navigate the trials of life, may we always remember to cling to our Great Physician, **Jesus**, and let the spirit of faith guide our actions. Amen.

.

CHAPTER THREE

Empowering God's Mighty Men through Devotion and Discipline

Faith is more than a concept or mere belief; it is a living, active force. Just as the muscles in our body grow stronger with exercise, so does our faith grow stronger as we exercise it in our lives. The Bible says in **James 2:26 (KJV), "For as the body without the spirit is dead, so faith without works is dead also."** This emphasizes that our faith, if left unexercised, becomes ineffective and dormant.

Faith is indeed likened to a muscle. If we refrain from using it, it atrophies. We must be doers of the word, not just listeners. In **James 1:22 (KJV),** the Bible instructs, **"But be ye doers of the word, and not hearers only, deceiving your own selves."** Just like in a workout class where participants might be at different fitness levels, it's not about where you start but about the journey and the determination to grow stronger. Taking small steps in faith can lead to significant spiritual growth.

Gathering with like-minded believers for prayer, as described, can be a pivotal practice. Prayer strengthens our relationship with **God**, fortifies our faith, and brings unity among believers. We can be inspired by **Matthew**

18:20 (KJV) which says, "For where two or three are gathered together in my name, there am I in the midst of them."

Surrendering oneself to **God**, yielding our will, and offering our minds and hearts can be transformative. The act of submission and humility before **God** can bring about remarkable change in one's life. By letting the Holy Spirit take control, we are saying, as in **Proverbs 3:5-6 (KJV), "Trust in the LORD with all thine heart; and lean not unto thine own understanding. In all thy ways acknowledge him, and he shall direct thy paths."**

To truly be **God's Mighty Men** and women, we need to be cautious about our spiritual diet. **Jesus** declared in **John 6:54 (KJV), "Whoso eateth my flesh, and drinketh my blood, hath eternal life; and I will raise him up at the last day."** This speaks to the essential spiritual sustenance found in **Christ**'s teachings and in **His** sacrifice. Just as our physical bodies need proper nourishment to thrive, our souls require the nourishing truth of **God's** Word.

Faith, like a muscle, requires consistent effort, nurturing, and discipline to grow and flourish. As believers, we are called to exercise our faith actively, immerse ourselves in **God's** Word, and surround ourselves with a community that encourages spiritual growth. Through commitment, devotion, and a focused spiritual diet, we can rise as **God's Mighty Men** and women, shining **His** light in a world desperately in need of hope.

Developing the Muscle of Faith

The Christian life is often depicted as a journey. It's a walk of faith, trust in the unseen, and a continual battle against adversaries, both physical and spiritual. Central to this walk is the strength of our faith—the spiritual muscle that we exercise and develop as we navigate through life's challenges. But just as physical muscles require regular workouts to grow stronger, our faith too needs to be nurtured and strengthened.

The act of partaking in the communion, "drinking the blood and eating the flesh of **Jesus**," signifies immersing oneself in the Word of **God (John 6:53: "Then Jesus said unto them, Verily, verily, I say unto you, Except ye eat the flesh of the Son of man, and drink his blood, ye have no life in you.").** As believers deeply invest in **God's** Word, faith blossoms, growing more robust and profound.

However, like physical workouts, exercising our faith might be accompanied by pain. Often, these pains are not indicative of sickness but represent spiritual growth, much like how sore muscles signify progress after a workout. It's essential to recognize these moments as opportunities to trust **God** even more and rely on **His** strength. Our trials and tribulations act as the resistance against which our faith muscle is exercised.

In **Hebrews 11:1**, we are told, **"Now faith is the substance of things hoped for, the evidence of things**

not seen." Faith is trusting in what we cannot see. Sometimes, this means trusting even when our circumstances seem contrary to our beliefs or when our prayers appear unanswered. Persistent trust and belief, even in the face of adversity, is the essence of exercising our faith.

An essential aspect of exercising our faith is our response to physical ailments or adversities. The Bible reminds us in **Ephesians 6:17** that the Word of **God** is the **"sword of the Spirit."** Armed with this sword, believers can confront adversities and challenges head-on, not in their strength but with the divine power that **God** provides.

Miraculous healings, like the testimonies of faith healers, may sometimes seem instantaneous. But more often than not, healing, deliverance, or any answer to prayer requires persistent faith, a relentless spirit, and an unyielding trust in **God's** timing. As **James 5:15** states, **"And the prayer of faith shall save the sick, and the Lord shall raise him up; and if he have committed sins, they shall be forgiven him."**

The journey of faith is one of endurance, resilience, and spiritual growth. It's a path where believers are called to exercise their faith muscles continually. By immersing oneself in the Word of **God** and trusting Him despite adversities, believers can develop a faith that can move mountains and overcome any challenge. In the battles of life, armed with the sword of the Spirit, **God's Mighty Men** and women are poised to triumph, ever punching the devil in the face, not by might nor by power but by the Spirit of the **Lord**.

A Reflection on God's Servitude and Victory

The strength and valor of the faithful, under **God's** guidance, is a remarkable testament to the profound impact of unwavering belief. The journey of every believer, as described in the Scriptures, provides ample evidence of how one's faith, even when confronted with overwhelming odds, remains a powerful force.

"So then faith cometh by hearing, and hearing by the word of God." (Romans 10:17, KJV)

Faith is not merely a passive acceptance but a call to action, a relentless pursuit of **God's** promise even when the road ahead seems treacherous. The Bible is replete with tales of those who, even in their weakest moments, embodied this spirit of determination, fueled by their faith. For instance, think of the times you feel defeated. Do you surrender to these feelings, or do you find strength in your faith, acting healed even when you're not, or feeling victorious even when circumstances suggest otherwise? It's essential to wear the armor of faith in every trial.

"But without faith it is impossible to please him: for he that cometh to God must believe that he is, and that he is a rewarder of them that diligently seek him." (Hebrews 11:6, KJV)

The story of Smith Wigglesworth serves as a powerful testament to this faith. As described, when faced with the physical evidence of death, Wigglesworth, with unwavering faith, demanded life in the name of **Jesus**. Three times he demanded, and on the third, his faith manifested in the miraculous. Such fervent belief in **God's** promise, even in the face of skepticism and doubt, is an inspiration for all.

Unbelief can be a debilitating force. It sows the seeds of doubt and undermines the foundations of our faith. Yet, it is vital to remember that **God's** creations are not accidental. When we feel insignificant, it is essential to remember the omnipotence of **God** and **His** plan for us.

"For I know the plans I have for you, declares the Lord, plans for welfare and not for evil, to give you a future and a hope." (Jeremiah 29:11, KJV)

King Saul's tale is a cautionary one, showcasing how pride and a departure from faith can lead to one's downfall. The allure of becoming "somebody," of elevating oneself above others, can lead even the most faithful astray. The humble realization that we are but instruments of **His** divine plan, always ready to serve, keeps us grounded in our faith.

Material desires, like Rolex watches or earthly treasures, pale in comparison to the eternal rewards of heaven. As believers, we must remember that the treasures of this world are fleeting. Our eyes should always be fixed on the eternal prize that awaits in heaven.

"Lay not up for yourselves treasures upon earth, where moth and rust doth corrupt, and where thieves break through and steal: But lay up for yourselves

treasures in heaven, where neither moth nor rust doth corrupt, and where thieves do not break through nor steal." (Matthew 6:19-20, KJV)

The **Mighty Men** of faith, from the Scriptures to modern-day testimonies, illuminate the path for every believer. They highlight the importance of unwavering belief, humility, and servitude in the face of worldly temptations and challenges. By reflecting on their journeys, believers can find renewed strength and inspiration to walk steadfastly on the path **God** has set before them, always cherishing the eternal rewards of heaven over transient earthly treasures.

A Call to Spiritual Warriorship

In the vast expanse of humanity's history, few matters carry the weight and significance of the eternal soul. **"For what shall it profit a man, if he shall gain the whole world, and lose his own soul?" (Mark 8:36 KJV)**. It's an age-old query that draws us to ponder the true essence of life's purpose. As believers, our ultimate mission becomes evident: winning souls.

Society's snares have ensnared many. Materialism's allure, often mistaken for genuine wealth and happiness, distracts us from our **God**-given calling. The Apostle Paul aptly articulates this growth from spiritual infancy to maturity, stating, **"When I was a child, I spake as a child, I understood as a child, I thought as a child: but**

when I became a man, I put away childish things." (1 Corinthians 13:11 KJV).

Today, there is an urgent clarion call for the "**Mighty Men** and women" to arise. This is not a summons for physical might but for spiritual valor. It's a plea to break free from distractions, worldly desires, and to pursue **Christ** with an unrelenting passion. For we are reminded**,** **"For we wrestle not against flesh and blood, but against principalities, against powers, against the rulers of the darkness of this world, against spiritual wickedness in high places." (Ephesians 6:12 KJV).** Our real enemy is not the people or the things of this world but the spiritual darkness that seeks to ensnare us.

Consider David, a young shepherd who faced Goliath, a seemingly invincible foe. Armed with divine assurance, David boldly declared**, "Thou comest to me with a sword, and with a spear, and with a shield: but I come to thee in the name of the LORD of hosts, the God of the armies of Israel, whom thou hast defied." (1 Samuel 17:45 KJV).** Goliath's pride and arrogance blinded him from seeing the true power of **God** at work.

Our journey as believers is marked by heroes and champions—those who stand as testaments of **God's** grace and power. Fathers are encouraged to be their daughter's hero, embodying **Christ**'s love, for **"The just man walketh in his integrity: his children are blessed after him." (Proverbs 20:7 KJV).** Families need pillars of faith who will intercede and war in the spiritual realms for their loved ones, just as **Christ** intercedes for us.

It is essential to recognize that our journey isn't about self-glorification but about magnifying **Christ**. The real treasures are not monetary but are discovered in the depths of our relationship with **God**. For the path to true riches is through sacrifice, faith, and utter dependence on **Him.** As Paul asserts, **"But my God shall supply all your need according to his riches in glory by Christ Jesus." (Philippians 4:19 KJV).**

In , the call for the "**Mighty Men** and women" is a call to spiritual warriorship, to stand firm against the wiles of the enemy, to be champions of faith, and to be beacons of **Christ**'s love in this world. As we heed this call, let us always remember that in our own strength we are nothing, but with **God**, we are more than conquerors. **"I can do all things through Christ which strengtheneth me." (Philippians 4:13 KJV).**

A Testament to Faith and Perseverance

In the ancient days of Israel, tales of men and women of **God** who stood firm in their faith echo through time. These are people who, despite adversities and challenges, remained unwavering in their commitment to the **Lord**, reminiscent of the Biblical account of David and his **Mighty Men**. They faced giants, vast armies, and seemingly insurmountable odds. Yet, their trust in **God's** promises saw them through. Such stories not only inspire but also challenge believers to step into their **God**-ordained destiny.

"And these all, having obtained a good report through faith, received not the promise." (Hebrews 11:39, KJV)

It's easy for one to judge, but the true heart of a believer is not in condemnation but in edification. This is not about inflated ego or mere words, but about action, resilience, and an earnest desire to guide fellow believers from one point of spiritual maturity to the next. Like teachers of faith and verity, as the Scripture says in **1 Timothy 2:7 (KJV): "Whereunto I am ordained a preacher, and an apostle, (I speak the truth in Christ, and lie not;) a teacher of the Gentiles in faith and verity."** The goal is to bring them to a place where they radiate the glory of **God** so powerfully that even adversities tremble at their presence.

The adversary, the devil, never desires for believers to walk in this fullness. Yet, with a heart anchored in praise and joy, believers can defy all odds. "...**Resist the devil, and he will flee from you." (James 4:7b, KJV)** And so, with a heart full of praise, and an unwavering spirit, believers can be a beacon of hope and healing, unafraid to lay hands on the sick and command healing in the name of **Jesus**.

"And these signs shall follow them that believe; In my name shall they cast out devils; they shall speak with new tongues; They shall take up serpents; and if they drink any deadly thing, it shall not hurt them; they shall lay hands on the sick, and they shall recover." (Mark 16:17-18, KJV)

There are countless testimonies, of believers overcoming by faith in **Jesus Christ**. Such testimonies emphasize that **God's** provision and favor are not just tales of old, but contemporary stories of **His** faithfulness. Like the Psalms declares, **"Except the LORD build the house, they labour in vain that build it: except the LORD keep the city, the watchman waketh but in vain." (Psalm 127:1, KJV)**

God's Mighty Men and women of today are those who stand firm in their faith, defy the norms, and walk in divine favor. They are vessels through which the Holy Spirit works, not merely in church pulpits but in everyday situations, be it at home, the marketplace, or even a store. As believers, let us aspire to be such vessels, living testimonies of **God's** goodness, proclaiming **His** name wherever we go, and constantly shining **His** light in a world desperately in need of hope.

Proclaiming the Word with Conviction

"For the word of God is quick, and powerful, and sharper than any two-edged sword, piercing even to the dividing asunder of soul and spirit, and of the joints and marrow, and is a discerner of the thoughts and intents of the heart." - Hebrews 4:12 (KJV)

Life's journey isn't about preaching, it's about living the Word. For over four decades, I've lived the embodiment of **Christ**'s teachings. When one is filled with the Holy

Spirit, they cannot help but share the message. This is reminiscent of what **Jesus** said: **"... out of the abundance of the heart the mouth speaketh." - Matthew 12:34b (KJV)**

During an ordinary day at Lowe's, an encounter with a young man named Blake epitomized this experience. Even in mundane moments, the spirit moves and prompts us to witness. **"And he said unto them, Go ye into all the world, and preach the gospel to every creature." - Mark 16:15 (KJV)**

Sometimes, people may be surrounded by the word yet not fully embrace it, like Blake whose father was a pastor from a denomination that didn't truly preach the essence of **Jesus**. Nevertheless, our duty remains the same: to share, to witness, and to bring the love of **Jesus** into every interaction. As said in Proverbs, **"The fruit of the righteous is a tree of life; and he that winneth souls is wise." - Proverbs 11:30 (KJV)**

What resides in our hearts will undoubtedly reflect in our actions and words. If one finds negativity pouring out, it's not counseling or medication that is needed, but rather the Gospel. This ties back to Romans: **"So then faith cometh by hearing, and hearing by the word of God." - Romans 10:17 (KJV)**

It's essential to approach others with understanding and compassion rather than judgment. Our mission isn't to castigate but to elevate, to help our brethren find the path to victory through **Christ**. As Paul wrote, **"To the weak became I as weak, that I might gain the weak: I am**

made all things to all men, that I might by all means save some." - 1 Corinthians 9:22 (KJV)

Conclusively, every individual is on a unique spiritual journey. We, as **God's Mighty Men**, are called to assist, guide, and spread the undying love of **Jesus Christ**. In every encounter, in every conversation, the Word should be at the forefront, guiding our hearts and tongues. Our commitment to this mission defines us and ensures that the love of **Christ** is perpetually echoed in every corner of the world. Amen.

"But ye shall receive power, after that the Holy Ghost is come upon you: and ye shall be witnesses unto me both in Jerusalem, and in all Judaea, and in Samaria, and unto the uttermost part of the earth." - Acts 1:8 (KJV)

The Modern Disconnection and Its Biblical Roots"

"Proclaim ye this among the Gentiles; Prepare war, wake up the Mighty Men, let all the men of war draw near; let them come up." - Joel 3:9 KJV

This verse from the book of Joel beckons the "**Mighty Men**" to awake and rise. This scripture isn't just a call to a physical warfare, but symbolically it speaks to the spiritual awakening and rise of strong leaders and devout followers of **God**. So, it begs the question: where are today's **Mighty Men** of faith?

A staggering 90% of the men in the United States profess a belief in **God**, and five out of six identify as Christians. Yet, only 35% regularly attend church alongside their spouses. Consequently, on any given Sunday in America, merely one out of every five women is accompanied by her husband at church. Such statistics highlight a noticeable disconnection between men and their active participation in the church. This phenomenon is uniquely observed in the Christian faith, for in other major world religions such as Buddhism, Hinduism, and Islam, men consistently outnumber women in religious congregations and practices.

Why does this anomaly exist? Was the scenario different during **Jesus**' time, or in the early days of Christianity?

To understand this disconnect, we should observe the representation of men in the Bible. Consider Jacob and Esau, twin brothers with vastly different personas. The Bible says, **"And the boys grew: and Esau was a cunning hunter, a man of the field; and Jacob was a plain man, dwelling in tents." - Genesis 25:27 KJV**. Jacob was a homemaker, a cook, smooth-skinned, while Esau was a rugged, hairy hunter. While one might have been suited for a magazine extolling the virtues of outdoor life, the other could be seen as a model for a hunting Magazine. Yet, **God** used both, showcasing that masculinity isn't monolithic.

The central message isn't about a man's physical strength or his ability to hunt, but about his heart and his relationship with **God**. Yet, the majority of men portrayed in the Bible might feel out of place in modern churches.

So, what has changed over time that has caused this shift away from church for so many men? Is it societal definitions of masculinity? Has the church's approach evolved in a way that doesn't resonate with men as it once did?

The challenge for the modern church is to bridge this gap, ensuring that it remains a place where all individuals, regardless of their gender or interests, feel a sense of belonging and connection to the Divine.

The Bible's call in Joel 3:9 for **Mighty Men** to awaken serves as a reminder of the importance of active faith and leadership. While the disconnect between men and church is evident in today's society, especially in Christianity, the essence of biblical masculinity is about heart, strength of character, and connection to **God**. The church's task, now more than ever, is to reaffirm this and reestablish itself as a space that resonates with everyone, ensuring that all can find their place within its walls.

A Study of Masculine Faith in Scriptures

The presence and narrative of **Jesus**' ministry has had an undeniable draw for men, clearly illustrated throughout the pages of the Bible. One only has to glance at the multitude he fed to comprehend this magnetic pull. **"And they that had eaten were about five thousand men,**

beside women and children" (Matthew 14:21, KJV). It's not an intent to undervalue the roles of women or children but a highlight of the powerful attraction **Jesus** had among men.

This emphasis on men's participation serves to portray the magnitude of **Jesus**' reach. In an era where society counted men in its headcounts, **Jesus**' ministry demonstrated immense influence. **"And there were added unto them about three thousand souls" (Acts 2:41, KJV)** at Pentecost, a significant event where the Holy Spirit was poured out.

Jesus had a remarkable strategy. **He** decided, "I'm going to find 12 men and I'm going to take over the world." The individuals he chose were not the traditional religious leaders of the day. They were men of the earth, like farmers and fishermen. Their authentic, unfiltered nature is evident when we learn that they were the kind who had, on occasion, indulged in strong language. These men, with their raw human tendencies, were attracted powerfully to **Jesus**' teachings.

Their genuine nature also meant that disputes arose. The Bible speaks of confrontations between Paul and Peter, which were of significant intensity. **"But when Peter was come to Antioch, I withstood him to the face, because he was to be blamed" (Galatians 2:11, KJV).** Such confrontations might seem shocking, especially between pillars of early Christianity, but they serve to show that these were real men with real emotions and convictions.

The overarching message here is the need for strong, devoted men in the body of **Christ**. Families and communities benefit when men lead with faith and conviction. Young boys, in particular, seek role models, often finding them in the men around them. To truly act like men of **God**, the scripture provides guidance. Paul writes in **1 Corinthians, "Watch ye, stand fast in the faith, quit you like men, be strong. Let all your things be done with charity" (1 Corinthians 16:13-14, KJV).** This passage not only encourages men to be vigilant and strong in faith but also emphasizes the importance of love in all actions.

The Bible, particularly presents a vivid portrait of men's role in the ministry of **Jesus Christ**. From farmers to fishermen, the scriptures highlight the real, raw, and powerful impact of genuine men on the spread of the Gospel. As role models for younger generations and pillars for their families, men are called to "act like men," grounding themselves in strength, faith, and above all, love. The scriptures serve as a timeless guide for all men to become the **Mighty Men** in **Christ** that our world so desperately needs.

The Call to True Manhood in Scripture

The call to manhood in the biblical sense is one that is both profound and essential in understanding the relationship between **God** and **His** children. The Bible is replete with exhortations for men to "act like men," and these directives have profound implications for how

Christian men should conduct themselves in their daily lives.

"Watch ye, stand fast in the faith, quit you like men, be strong." (1 Corinthians 16:13, KJV)

The essence of the exhortation is clear: Men, in their divine role, are called to be pillars of strength, leading with purpose and intention. But what does it truly mean to "act like a man"?

Leading, Not Following

To "act like a man" does not imply a derogatory stance towards women. Rather, it underscores the distinct leadership role men are ordained to take on, particularly within the family unit. Men are called to be spiritual leaders, providing direction and taking responsibility for their households.

"But if any provide not for his own, and specially for those of his own house, he hath denied the faith, and is worse than an infidel." (1 Timothy 5:8, KJV)

Understanding and Honor Towards Women

While the Bible does refer to women as the **"weaker vessel"** in **1 Peter 3**, it is crucial to note that this doesn't diminish women's value or significance in **God's** eyes. This statement emphasizes the physical distinction, urging men to care for, cherish, and honor women.

"Likewise, ye husbands, dwell with them according to knowledge, giving honour unto the wife, as unto the weaker vessel, and as being heirs together of the grace

of life; that your prayers be not hindered." (1 Peter 3:7, KJV)

Men are called to treat women with understanding and respect, recognizing that both genders, though distinct, are equally valued in **God's** kingdom.

Stepping Up in Spiritual Responsibility

A man's strength is not merely physical but extends to emotional, mental, and spiritual realms. Men are exhorted to nurture their spiritual lives, ensuring they're not the "weaker vessel" in their relationship with **God**.

"And thou shalt love the Lord thy God with all thy heart, and with all thy soul, and with all thy might." (Deuteronomy 6:5, KJV)

Avoiding Needless Drama

Men, as leaders, are also called to demonstrate maturity by avoiding unnecessary conflicts and drama. This doesn't mean suppressing emotions but expressing them healthily and constructively.

"He that is slow to anger is better than the Mighty; and he that ruleth his spirit than he that taketh a city." (Proverbs 16:32, KJV)

God's call for men to be **Mighty** is a multi-faceted directive that emphasizes leadership, understanding, spiritual strength, and maturity. It's a **divine blueprint**, urging men to live with purpose, integrity, and unwavering faith. When men answer this call, they not only draw closer to **God** but also set a powerful example for future generations, underscoring the timeless relevance of **God's** word in shaping true manhood.

A Call to True Masculinity

The biblical model of manhood is consistently clear about the characteristics that define a **God**ly man. The scripture advocates for men to rise above the challenges of the world, shunning behaviors that are unbecoming of their divine mandate. This teaching examines the true essence of what it means to be "**God's Mighty Men**" by delving into the behaviors they must shun and those they must uphold, all while referencing the time-honored of the Bible.

"Watch ye, stand fast in the faith, quit you like men, be strong." (1 Corinthians 16:13 KJV)

Act Like a Man

To embrace true manhood is to rise above dramatic outbursts, ensuring that one's presence does not cause discomfort or fear within the household or community. This calls for a man to be calm, controlled, and considerate in demeanor.

"For the fruit of the Spirit is in all goodness and righteousness and truth;" (Ephesians 5:9 KJV)

When filled with the Holy Spirit, a man is equipped to manage anger and frustrations. The Spirit aids in molding a kind, considerate, and holy nature. Being unkind is a deviation from holiness, as **God**ly attributes emphasize kindness.

Shun Animalistic Desires

The scripture is rich with instances where man's beastly nature is admonished. King David, after committing adultery, recognized his descent into such behavior, saying: **"Behold, I was shapen in iniquity; and in sin did my mother conceive me." (Psalm 51:5 KJV)**

King Nebuchadnezzar, on the other hand, was reduced to an animalistic state as a consequence of his arrogance and separation from **God**.

"And he was driven from the sons of men; and his heart was made like the beasts, and his dwelling was with the wild asses: they fed him with grass like oxen, and his body was wet with the dew of heaven; till he knew that the most high God ruled in the kingdom of men, and that he appointeth over it whomsoever he will." (Daniel 5:21 KJV)

A **God**ly man is called to rise above selfish desires and animalistic tendencies. True manhood requires a man to be selfless, considerate, and to uphold manners that reflect respect and love for others.

Move Beyond Childhood

The transition from boyhood to manhood is a significant one in the scripture. The Apostle Paul speaks of this transition in 1 Corinthians, saying:

"When I was a child, I spake as a child, I understood as a child, I thought as a child: but when I became a man, I put away childish things." (1 Corinthians 13:11 KJV)

A **God**ly man is called to leave the dependencies and immaturities of boyhood behind. **He** must recognize that his responsibilities have grown, and his behavior should reflect this growth.

True manhood, as reflected in the teachings of the scripture, is a balance of strength, wisdom, and compassion. **God's Mighty Men** are called to be pillars of their communities, reflecting **God's** love and righteousness in their actions. As we navigate the challenges of our times, let every man strive to embody these virtues, living not as mere men but as **God's** chosen representatives on earth.

A Call to Spiritual Vigilance

"When I was a child, I spake as a child, I understood as a child, I thought as a child: but when I became a man, I put away childish things." - 1 Corinthians 13:11 (KJV)

The aforementioned scripture from the book of Corinthians vividly encapsulates the transformation from the naiveté of childhood to the maturity of manhood. A man's responsibility is profound, and it goes beyond mere physical growth; it encompasses spiritual and emotional maturity. This teaching delves into the essence of being one of **God's Mighty Men**.

Many find themselves trapped in an extended phase of immaturity. They refrain from assuming responsibility and often hide behind the cloak of youth. But as aptly noted, being young is a fleeting phase, yet one can remain immature indefinitely. Such a state is not what **God** intends for **His** men. To be clear, acting like a man is not about undermining women, nor is it about adopting beastly behaviors or retaining the immaturity of youth. Instead, it is about stepping up, being watchful, and taking responsibility.

Three predominant themes emerge when we discuss the concept of acting like a man, especially as seen in the biblical context:

The Military Vigilance:
Watch ye, stand fast in the faith, quit you like men, be strong. - 1 Corinthians 16:13 (KJV). This scripture hints at the military rigor that men are to adopt. Being watchful, in this context, relates to being vigilant, akin to watchmen on the walls of an ancient city. These watchmen, as protective figures, would ensure that no danger befell the city and its inhabitants. Similarly, **God's Mighty Men** are called to be spiritually vigilant, guarding their families and communities from spiritual

adversaries and dangers.

Assuming Responsibility:
Men are called to prioritize their families. This is evident in scriptures such as **But if any provide not for his own, and specially for those of his own house, he hath denied the faith, and is worse than an infidel. - 1 Timothy 5:8 (KJV).** Providing here isn't merely about physical provisions, but also emotional, spiritual, and mental support. Recognizing and admitting one's mistakes and shortcomings is part of this responsibility. It signifies growth and the commitment to rectifying errors.

Spiritual Fortitude:
Being strong in faith and moral conviction is pivotal. **Finally, my brethren, be strong in the Lord, and in the power of his might. - Ephesians 6:10 (KJV).** This scripture underscores the importance of deriving strength from the Almighty, standing firm in faith, and not faltering in the face of challenges.

In, being one of **God's Mighty Men** is not about conforming to societal expectations of masculinity. It is about spiritual vigilance, responsibility, and fortitude. It is about being the protective watchman, the responsible provider, and the spiritual warrior, rooted in faith and guided by the Almighty's wisdom. It is a call to rise, embrace maturity, and stand as a beacon of **God's** love, strength, and purpose.

A Call to Be Watchmen in a Tempestuous Age

"Put on the whole armour of God, that ye may be able to stand against the wiles of the devil." - Ephesians 6:11 (KJV)

In a time where the very fabric of our homes is being torn apart by unseen forces, the call to be vigilant has never been more pertinent. As I pen down these words, I recall my own journey. As a pastor, husband, father, and grandfather, I have faced my own share of tumultuous storms. Yet, amidst the chaos, one thing remains constant: The **Lord**'s assurance and **His** call for **His** men to rise as watchmen.

Families today, more than ever, find themselves in the crosshairs of spiritual, emotional, and societal struggles. As a father of five and grandfather to one, I've felt the weight of **God's** responsibility. I've witnessed the fractures that threaten to break the bond of family. The voices of doubt, despair, and temptation often whisper, attempting to steer us away from our divine purpose.

"Be sober, be vigilant; because your adversary the devil, as a roaring lion, walketh about, seeking whom he may devour:" - 1 Peter 5:8 (KJV)

In today's digital age, our roles as protectors expand beyond the physical realm. Media and the internet often serve as conduits for negativity and temptation, making our responsibility even more essential. We must be guardians of not only our homes but also of the content that permeates the walls of our sanctuaries.

Our children, the next generation, rely on us for guidance. The example of Eli and his sons from the Old Testament is a sobering reminder. The scripture recounts, **"And the sons of Eli were sons of Belial; they knew not the LORD." - 1 Samuel 2:12 (KJV).** The Bible tells us Eli's sons were termed 'worthless' because he failed to guide them away from wickedness. As leaders of our households, we must not be complacent. Instead, we should act as pillars of righteousness, guiding and guarding our families against harm.

Being a watchman entails actively overseeing our children's choices, from the music they listen to, to the language they adopt. If we do not step up and intervene, if we do not "restrain" them as Eli failed to do, we risk letting malevolence seep into their lives.

"Train up a child in the way he should go: and when he is old, he will not depart from it." - Proverbs 22:6 (KJV)

In these challenging times, it is our sacred duty to stand tall as **God's Mighty Men**. To don the armor of **God** and ward off the malevolent forces that threaten our families. We are called to be watchmen, vigilant guardians of our homes and hearts. Let us strive daily, fervently praying and actively safeguarding our families, ensuring that our legacy stands strong in the **Lord**'s light. Amen.

CHAPTER FOUR

Being a Watchman in a Shifting Culture

In a rapidly changing world, it's essential for men to stand as watchmen over their families, upholding the biblical principles and values that have guided generations. Drawing from the Bible, this teaching underscores the importance of men taking an active role in the spiritual nurturing of their families.

"But if the watchman see the sword come, and blow not the trumpet, and the people be not warned; if the sword come, and take any person from among them, he is taken away in his iniquity; but his blood will I require at the watchman's hand." - Ezekiel 33:6 KJV

Being a watchman is more than just an observatory role. It entails taking action, providing guidance, and sometimes correcting course. Fathers, especially, play a pivotal role. In a culture where distractions abound, it's essential for men to step up and guide their children, particularly sons. Boys naturally seek male figures to emulate, and when righteous men set an example, boys will inevitably follow.

The scripture reminds us, **"Train up a child in the way he should go: and when he is old, he will not depart**

from it." - Proverbs 22:6 KJV

But it's not just about being present; it's about standing firm in one's faith. One should not sway or alter their beliefs to fit into a shifting society. Instead, let the unchanging word of **God** be the anchor.

"Therefore, my beloved brethren, be ye stedfast, unmoveable, always abounding in the work of the Lord, forasmuch as ye know that your labour is not in vain in the Lord." - 1 Corinthians 15:58 KJV

In other words, don't adjust your theology to mirror your behavior or fit into contemporary standards. Hold tight to convictions. Remember that the Word of **God** is meant to be our guiding light in times of cultural shifts, reminding us to return to holiness, purity, and a steadfast walk with **God**.

Furthermore, all actions, corrections, and teachings must be rooted in love. Scripture warns against using wrath, especially within the familial unit, as it won't produce the desired righteousness.

"For the wrath of man worketh not the righteousness of God." - James 1:20 KJV

As fathers and leaders, showing love even in correction is vital. Emotions may surge, especially when witnessing loved ones stray from righteous paths, but anger won't bring them back. Only love can do that.

In , being **God's Mighty** man in today's age is about being a vigilant watchman, standing unwaveringly in faith and guiding one's family with love. In a world full of fleeting trends and altering standards, the Word of **God** remains unchanged. Let it be the compass guiding every man, ensuring that they remain steadfast in their faith, leading their families toward righteousness and holiness.

The Power of Unyielding Love

Throughout scripture, **God** has consistently demonstrated **His** immense love for **His** creation. **His** love is relentless, unfathomable, and unwavering, even when faced with humanity's frequent shortcomings. One of the most striking examples of **God's Mighty Men** in the Bible can be seen in their relentless commitment to love and righteousness, often against all odds and opposition.

While our emotions are vast and diverse, it's essential to remember the true nature and repercussions of our actions, especially when propelled by wrath. As **James 1:20** states, **"For the wrath of man worketh not the righteousness of God."** It's clear from this scripture that unbridled anger, especially when expressed through screaming, will not align with **God's** divine will or produce the righteousness **He** seeks.

The Message Bible, a modern translation that seeks to

capture the nuance of the original texts, illuminates this theme even further by encouraging actions to be rooted in love. Specifically, it says, **"Let all that you do be done in love." An unyielding, undeterred love - love that does not stop, even when faced with adversity or heartbreak.** The Message Bible reiterates this sentiment, saying, **"Love without stopping."**

Life will inevitably present us with challenges, heartbreaks, and situations where our patience is tested. Loved ones may make choices we don't understand or agree with, and moments may arise where it seems easier to succumb to anger rather than approach with love. However, as believers, we're called to emulate **God's** unyielding love. Screaming, ranting, and other forms of violent expressions do not lead to righteousness. Instead, as **1 Corinthians 16:14** beautifully sums up, **"Let all your things be done with charity."**

It's vital for every individual, whether in a marriage, family, or other relationships, to remember this **God**ly call. It's easy to focus on disagreements and imperfections. However, to mirror **God's** love in our lives requires us to love without ceasing. As **1 John 4:7-8 (KJV)** says, **"Beloved, let us love one another: for love is of God; and every one that loveth is born of God, and knoweth God. He that loveth not knoweth not God; for God is love."**

God's Mighty Men and women are those who stand firm in their commitment to love unyieldingly. Just as **God's** love for us never wavers, we are called to demonstrate this same kind of love in our interactions with others. In a world where anger and division can seem omnipresent, it is the unwavering love, rooted deeply in scripture and **God's** nature, that has the true power to bring forth the righteousness of **God**. The essence of our faith and our calling is, simply put, to "love without stopping."

Reflections on Life and the Sacredness of Service

"And as it is appointed unto men once to die, but after this the judgment:" (Hebrews 9:27 KJV)

When we wander through the halls of old museums, we are often drawn to artworks that capture the meditative monks, contemplating a skull held in their hands. To the uninitiated observer, such imagery seems dark and macabre. Yet, on a deeper level, it signifies a profound reflection on mortality. For in that skull, the monk sees not just the remains of another but an image of his own eventual fate. As the scriptures say, **"For dust thou art, and unto dust shalt thou return." (Genesis 3:19 KJV).**

Strong men, revered and looked up to for their strength and vitality, eventually grow old. Their vigor diminishes, and they, too, meet the same fate that awaits us all. The inevitability of death is a shared human experience, one that transcends status, ability, and achievement. For as the wise King Solomon said in Ecclesiastes, **"Then shall the dust return to the earth as it was: and the spirit shall return unto God who gave it." (Ecclesiastes 12:7 KJV).**

But does recognizing this reality mean we resign ourselves to despair? Certainly not. For while the mortality of life is undeniable, the purpose and meaning we derive from it, especially within the framework of faith, give it immense value. There exists no true division between the sacred and the secular in the life of a believer. Every act, every profession, every mundane task can be infused with sacredness when done unto **Christ**.

"And whatsoever ye do, do it heartily, as to the Lord, and not unto men;" (Colossians 3:23 KJV). Be it a preacher, a missionary, a doctor, or a construction worker, when one works with the intent of glorifying **God**, every action is sacred.

A personal revelation of this came not through a profound spiritual experience, but through the harsh realities of life. In the midst of an ordinary day, the sudden death of our little four-year-old girl made clear the transient nature of life. That despite our plans, aspirations, or how closely we love our family, death remains an inescapable truth. Yet, this realization shouldn't lead to hopelessness, but instead a renewed focus on living a life filled with purpose and intent, aligned with the will of **Christ**.

In , reflecting upon our own mortality can be the catalyst for a deeper understanding of life's value and purpose. We are reminded that every moment is a gift and that each action, when dedicated to the glory of **God**, can transform the mundane into the sacred. By recognizing our own eventual fate, we can live with more purpose, ensuring that our lives resonate with meaning, not just for ourselves, but in the service of the Almighty.

"For to me to live is Christ, and to die is gain." (Philippians 1:21 KJV).

A Reflection on Divine Investment and Purpose

"I have fought a good fight, I have finished my course, I have kept the faith." - 2 Timothy 4:7 (KJV)

Throughout our life's journey, challenges arise that test our faith, strength, and determination. These trials mold us into the **Mighty** warriors that **God** intended for us to become. To be strong, courageous, intelligent, and ultimately successful is the path many yearn to tread, and it often comes with sacrifice. Like the allure of romance, when we fall deeply in love and lose it, we are reminded of the fragility of our existence and the fleeting nature of earthly treasures.

"Set your affection on things above, not on things on the earth." - Colossians 3:2 (KJV)

The incessant noise of the media often drowns our introspective thoughts. Thus, the importance of introspection, of taking moments to contemplate one's own mortality, can't be understated. At the end of it all, we must ask: Where have we invested our time, resources, and energy?

In the realm of academia, as illustrated by many colleges, there's an immense pool of knowledge. But within this sea, where does **God** fit in? When peers question your newfound Christian faith, the realization comes that in the light of eternity much of the modern education is meaningless. Instead, the focus should shift from the temporal to the eternal.

"Lay not up for yourselves treasures upon earth, where moth and rust doth corrupt, and where thieves break through and steal: But lay up for yourselves treasures in heaven, where neither moth nor rust doth corrupt, and where thieves do not break through nor steal." - Matthew 6:19-20 (KJV)

This world, with all its allure and promise, is temporary. Investing in it alone would be folly. The adversary, ever cunning, seeks to divert our attention from the true treasures. To invest in one's **Godliness** is to invest in a treasure that remains uncorrupted. A commitment to personal growth in **Godliness** not only benefits oneself but ripples outward, touching the lives of spouses, children, and the broader church community.

"And beside this, giving all diligence, add to your faith virtue; and to virtue knowledge; And to knowledge temperance; and to temperance patience; and to patience Godliness; And to Godliness brotherly kindness; and to brotherly kindness charity." - 2 Peter 1:5-7 (KJV)

The question we must continually pose to ourselves is: Where are we placing our investments? Are we dedicating time and effort to foster our personal relationship with **God**, nurturing our family's spiritual growth, and serving our local church community?

In life's ebb and flow, where we choose to invest our resources will determine the legacy we leave behind. **God** calls **His Mighty Men** and women to a higher purpose, one that transcends earthly desires and focuses on eternal rewards. By understanding the true essence of investment - not in the fleeting treasures of this world but in **Godliness**, family, and community - we align ourselves with **God's** purpose. Let us be reminded always to set our sights not on what is seen but on the treasures that await in the Kingdom of Heaven. For in doing so, we truly become **God's Mighty** warriors, ever steadfast in faith and purpose.

Daily Bread and the Pursuit of Holiness

Throughout biblical scripture, there are countless reminders of man's purpose and his intimate relationship with **God**. A significant exemplar of this is found in the **Lord**'s Prayer, a foundation of Christian teaching and an insight into **Christ**'s perspective on human existence. When **Jesus** teaches his disciples this prayer, he emphasizes a life devoted to the honor and service of **God**, and it provides us with a guide to understand our own roles as **God's** servants on Earth.

One of the most debated parts of the **Lord**'s Prayer is the phrase, **"Give us this day our daily bread" (Matthew 6:11, KJV).** Many interpretations surround this line, often focusing on its literalness, longevity, or spiritual nuances. However, its core essence is a simple yet profound plea: **Lord**, provide us with what we need for today so that we can serve You and fulfill Your will.

This isn't a cry for prosperity, luxury, or a long-life's worth of provisions. Instead, it's a humble request for enough sustenance to continue the divine mission. **"And having food and raiment let us be therewith content" (1 Timothy 6:8, KJV)**. In essence, it articulates the true purpose of our existence: to glorify **God's** name, establish **His** kingdom, and ensure **His** will is done on Earth.

In the creation story, **God** commands Adam to spread **His** kingdom and ensure that the world aligns with **His** will. This divine mandate, sometimes referred to as the "creation commission," resonates throughout scriptures and emphasizes the divine purpose set before humanity:

"And God blessed them, and God said unto them, Be fruitful, and multiply, and replenish the earth, and subdue it: and have dominion over the fish of the sea, and over the fowl of the air, and over every living thing that moveth upon the earth" (Genesis 1:28, KJV).

When reflecting upon the Great Commission, it appears as a reiteration and expansion of this creation mandate, encompassing not just the Earth but our hearts, families, and communities. Every biblical commandment, whether for families, individuals, or communities, aligns with this goal of spreading **God's** dominion.

The scripture reminds us that this world is transient. **"And the world passeth away, and the lust thereof: but he that doeth the will of God abideth for ever" (1 John 2:17, KJV).** Our lives here are not meant for self-indulgence or hedonistic pursuits. Rather, Earth is our battleground, where we must constantly strive to ensure **God's** will prevails.

Our journey on Earth is short-lived, but its purpose is monumental. As **God's Mighty Men**, we're entrusted with the great responsibility of upholding **His** kingdom, ensuring **His** name remains sanctified, and fulfilling **His** will. Our prayers should always echo the essence of the **Lord**'s Prayer, seeking sustenance, guidance, and strength to continue this divine mission. Every morsel of bread, every breath we take, should be seen as a gift, fueling us in our battle to serve and glorify the Almighty.

Decline of Noble Leadership in Society

"For, behold, the Lord, the LORD of hosts, doth take away from Jerusalem and from Judah the stay and the staff, the whole stay of bread, and the whole stay of water, The Mighty man, and the man of war, the judge, and the prophet, and the prudent, and the ancient, The captain of fifty, and the honourable man, and the counsellor, and the cunning artificer, and the eloquent orator." (Isaiah 3:1-3, KJV)

As we dive into this study of **God's Mighty Men**, it's vital to understand the significance of leadership in society and its decline, especially when we look at Isaiah chapter three. The forewarning of judgment upon a nation is not just the removal of its essential supplies but also its noble men. The **Lord God**, in **His** divine wisdom, indicates that one of the harshest judgments **He** can enact upon a society is to strip it of its wise, honorable, and **Mighty Men**.

"And I will give children to be their princes, and babes shall rule over them. And the people shall be oppressed..." (Isaiah 3:4-5, KJV)

Fast-forwarding to our contemporary society, it's hard to deny the parallels. The lament is clear: where have the noble men gone? Why do we see the degradation of the image of leadership in our society? From media portrayals of fathers and leaders as inept and foolish to young men becoming more absorbed in trivialities than taking responsibility, there's an evident decline. The text's emphasis on the absence of the noble from leadership positions is poignant.

Reflecting upon the state of our nation today, one might discern that we are seeing Isaiah's words come to life. Men of virtue, strength, and wisdom appear to be a diminishing breed, replaced by those who are impressionable and whimsical. There's a marked contrast between the leadership that was revered in ancient times and what we often see now.

The lament on sitcoms mirrors a broader societal trend. The portrayal of fathers as lacking in wisdom, while children possess the answers, is more than just comedic relief; it signifies a shift in societal values and perceptions. Christian men, immersed in **God's** word, ought to be alarmed. Yet, many overlook this shift, suggesting a lack of grounding in the Scripture.

In , the decline of **God's Mighty Men** in our society is a cause for concern. If Isaiah's words offer any counsel, it's that the removal of noble leadership is a severe judgment. For a society to thrive, it requires strong, righteous, and wise leaders. The challenge for today's generation is to recognize this decline and aspire to rise to the noble call of leadership, grounded firmly in **God's** word.

"And he will be our peace when the Assyrians invade our land and march through our fortresses. We will raise against them seven shepherds, even eight commanders." (Micah 5:5, KJV)

Let us pray for a resurgence of such noble leaders in our land.

God's Mighty Men and the Power of His Word: A Reflection from the Book of Life

The journey of spiritual growth and seeking the Divine is as intricate as it is fascinating. Throughout history, the scriptures have illuminated the paths of countless individuals, directing them toward a life of righteousness, guidance, and profound understanding. One of the foundational elements of this divine journey is the word of **God** as detailed in the scriptures.

Brothers, we often become embroiled in the complexities of life, searching for answers in far-off places, when the solution lies right before us. It's the word of **God**. This word, this divine message, is our beacon.

A personal anecdote serves to amplify this point. My wife once relayed her experiences teaching a group of women. After emphasizing the importance of submitting to your husband as unto **Christ**, the whole woman's group revolted against her. They may not have agreed, but **God**s word is still **God**s word!

"So then faith cometh by hearing, and hearing by the word of God." - Romans 10:17 KJV

We need not ascend to the heavens or delve into the underworld. The path is simple, though not necessarily easy. Engage with the scriptures, associate with the virtuous, bond with your family around the teachings of **God**, and internalize **His** word.

However, this simplicity also becomes our accountability. On the final day of reckoning, we shall stand before the Almighty, and the ease of the path will become the weight of our responsibility.

"For the word of God is quick, and powerful, and sharper than any twoedged sword, piercing even to the dividing asunder of soul and spirit, and of the joints and marrow, and is a discerner of the thoughts and intents of the heart." - Hebrews 4:12 KJV

Now, referring to the scriptures, the societal reflections are uncanny. **"And the people will be oppressed each one by another and each one by his neighbor; the youth will storm against the elder and the inferior against the honorable."** This verse mirrors the very societal fabric we find ourselves embedded within today.

Verse 12, which mentions, **"Oh my people, their oppressors are children and women rule over them,"** is often misinterpreted as a portrayal of women in a negative light. However, the core message is about the order of society and the importance of leadership based on righteousness and understanding rather than mere positions of power. This reveals that men had forsaken their spiritual roles as the leaders in their homes.

"Let no man despise thy youth; but be thou an example of the believers, in word, in conversation, in charity, in spirit, in faith, in purity." - 1 Timothy 4:12 KJV

In the myriad complexities of life, the scriptures stand as a timeless beacon, guiding believers to lead lives rooted in understanding, love, and righteousness. We, as **God's Mighty Men**, have a responsibility to immerse ourselves in **His** word, for therein lies the path of true spiritual growth. Engaging with the word of **God** is not a mere act; it's a commitment to leading a life aligned with **His** divine teachings.

The Power of Commitment to His Word

The interwoven tapestry of human experience and divine guidance is eternally mesmerizing. Throughout the annals of history, holy scriptures have emerged as the lighthouses, shedding light on the intricate maze of life, guiding countless souls towards righteousness, understanding, and a life aligned with the divine. Central to this ethereal journey is the unwavering word of **God** as enshrined in the scriptures.

In the hustle and bustle of life, many a time, we find ourselves lost, searching in myriad corners for enlightenment. Yet, oftentimes, the answer is not in distant lands but right before our very eyes — the word of **God**. This divine directive serves as our guiding star. Spiritual evolution is not about performing magnificent deeds but about relentless engagement with the divine word.

"So then faith cometh by hearing, and hearing by the word of God." - Romans 10:17 KJV

From Deborah to Today's Generation

Throughout history, the scriptures have given us narratives of powerful men and women whose lives offer lessons for every generation. Among such biblical figures are the likes of Jezebel and Deborah. Their stories provide insight into the roles of women in the context of authority and leadership, and they pose questions that resonate with contemporary audiences.

Jezebel, as the scriptures depict, was a wicked woman who sought to usurp authority in a male-dominated society. The Bible in 1 Kings 21:25 describes her influence by saying, **"But there was none like unto Ahab, which did sell himself to work wickedness in the sight of the LORD, whom Jezebel his wife stirred up."** Jezebel represents a misuse of power and authority, driven by personal ambition and wicked intentions.

On the other hand, Deborah's story offers a stark contrast. She was a righteous leader, raised by **God** during a time when Israel needed guidance and direction. **Judges 4:4-5 (KJV)** elucidates, **"And Deborah, a prophetess, the wife of Lapidoth, she judged Israel at that time. And she dwelt under the palm tree of Deborah between Ramah and Bethel in mount Ephraim: and the children of Israel came up to her for judgment."** Deborah stands as a beacon of hope and strength, providing guidance to the nation when male leadership was lacking.

It could be surmised that Deborah's rise to leadership was a rebuke to the men of her time. Her leadership raises poignant questions about the roles and expectations of men and women in society. In the contemporary world, many young women express concerns about their futures in light of the behaviors and choices of their male counterparts. The dilemma of whether to remain single or settle for less than ideal partners resonates with many.

The legacy of one generation greatly influences the next. As it was with Israel, where a generation arose that **"did not know the Lord"** due to the failures of the preceding generation (**Judges 2:10 KJV: "And also all that generation were gathered unto their fathers: and there arose another generation after them, which knew not the LORD, nor yet the works which he had done for Israel"),** the same can be said of today's generation. While modern distractions may differ from those of biblical times, the essence of the struggle remains the same.

The lessons from these biblical figures implore us to

reflect on our own lives. It's crucial to understand that our lives are meant to be poured out in service to others, to our families, and to our church. The core of Christian teaching revolves around self-sacrifice, love, and commitment. It's not just about acknowledging **Christ** but living out **His** teachings in every facet of our lives.

God's Mighty Men and women from scriptures offer timeless lessons. The stories of Jezebel and Deborah remind us of the complexities of leadership, authority, and gender roles, lessons that are as relevant today as they were thousands of years ago. It's imperative for every generation to heed these lessons, building a legacy of righteousness, integrity, and love for the next generation. In doing so, we ensure that the light of **Christ** continues to shine brightly in a world that so desperately needs it.

The Role of Character in Spiritual Leadership

Throughout the annals of history, the elect people of **God** have played a pivotal role in the dissemination of the gospel message. The Book of Romans tells us, **"For whosoever shall call upon the name of the Lord shall be saved. How then shall they call on him in whom they have not believed? And how shall they believe in him of whom they have not heard? And how shall they hear without a preacher?" (Romans 10:13-14 KJV).** It is evident that there are those chosen by **God** who have yet to encounter the transformative power of the gospel message. And it falls upon the shoulders of those who have been called, equipped, and positioned to reach out.

I am reminded of the devout and dedicated individuals in the church, including the professional men who, despite their bustling schedules, prioritize sharing the good news. It is humbling to witness individuals who, regardless of their career achievements, prioritize the Kingdom's work. The impact they make is reminiscent of the Apostle Paul's words**: "I have planted, Apollos watered; but God gave the increase" (1 Corinthians 3:6 KJV).**

However, the most striking observation is their commitment not just to the external ministry but to the internal sanctification process. It brings to mind the imagery of the concentric circles of concern. At the core of these circles is the individual believer, striving to be more **Christ**-like. This idea, although seemingly counterintuitive, is profoundly Christian. The journey begins with self, as echoed in the scriptures: **"Thou shalt love thy neighbour as thyself" (Matthew 22:39 KJV).** The foundational step in influencing others for **Christ** is by allowing **Christ** to influence and transform us first.

There's profound wisdom in understanding that the greatest gift one can offer the world is a heart and life transformed by **Christ**. This resonates with **Romans 12:2**, which says, **"And be not conformed to this world: but be ye transformed by the renewing of your mind, that ye may prove what is that good, and acceptable, and perfect, will of God" (KJV).**

Moreover, the scriptures emphasize character, especially when considering leadership roles within the church. The epistles of Titus and Timothy are clear about this. An elder, or any church leader for that matter, should possess character traits that mirror **Christ**. As stated, **"If a man desire the office of a bishop, he desireth a good work. A bishop then must be blameless, the husband of one wife, vigilant, sober, of good behaviour, given to hospitality, apt to teach" (1 Timothy 3:1-2 KJV).** But these qualities should not just be limited to church leaders; they reflect the life every believer should aspire to live.

The call to be **God's Mighty Men** is not just about grand evangelistic endeavors. It's a call to cultivate an intimate relationship with **Christ** and allow that transformation to influence every sphere of our lives. It starts from within, with a dedication to personal spiritual growth, which subsequently radiates outward. As we prioritize character and Christlikeness, we become living epistles, drawing many more to the saving knowledge of our **Lord** and Savior, **Jesus Christ**.

Reflecting Christ in Marriage and Fatherhood

"Husbands, love your wives, even as Christ also loved the church, and gave himself for it;" (Ephesians 5:25 KJV)

It's paramount to understand that simply knowing the principles of marriage isn't the sole guarantee of its success. Indeed, if you're a man filled with the Holy Spirit, exhibiting the fruit of the spirit, you're on a solid foundation. **“But the fruit of the Spirit is love, joy, peace, longsuffering, gentleness, goodness, faith, meekness, temperance: against such there is no law.” (Galatians 5:22-23 KJV).** A union built on spiritual grounds is crucial, but so too is the understanding and application of marital principles.

The Bible gives clear directives about our priorities. A man's primary concern should be his wife's spiritual and emotional well-being. Just as **Christ** gave himself for the church, a husband should prioritize his wife's sanctification, **Godliness**, and prosperity. **“So ought men to love their wives as their own bodies. He that loveth his wife loveth himself.” (Ephesians 5:28 KJV).**

Some might object, asking, "What about my needs?" But here, the answer is evident: A man must die to his selfish desires. **Christ** exemplified this sacrifice; **“Greater love hath no man than this, that a man lay down his life for his friends.” (John 15:13 KJV).** It's an act of servitude, a testament of true manhood, to place one's family before oneself.

Children are, undeniably, a pivotal part of a family. However, they should not replace the affection and intimacy meant for a spouse. One of the profound ways a father can love his children is by loving their mother, for a stable marital relationship provides a bedrock for a child's emotional and spiritual growth.

The repercussions of neglect are far-reaching. A wife who's deprived of her husband's affection might inadvertently seek solace in her children, creating an imbalance in familial relationships. **"Can two walk together, except they be agreed?" (Amos 3:3 KJV).** It's imperative to keep the marital bond strong, ensuring that no part of the family fabric becomes unraveled.

A deep study of the Scriptures reveals how intricately **God** has woven **His** principles into every aspect of our lives. Taking Hebrews 10 as an example, we see the interweaving of Biblical truths, reminding us of the connectivity of **God's** commands.

Conclusively, a **God**ly man, reflecting **Christ** in his actions, ensures that his concentric circles of concern encompass his wife, children, the people of **God**, and the world. By doing so, he fulfills his divine calling, echoing the teachings of **Christ** and showcasing the Gospel's transformative power.

"Let your light so shine before men, that they may see your good works, and glorify your Father which is in heaven." (Matthew 5:16 KJV).

A Discourse on Faithfulness

"And the things that thou hast heard of me among many witnesses, the same commit thou to faithful men, who shall be able to teach others also." - 2 Timothy 2:2 (KJV)

Understanding the depths and significance of this scripture from 2 Timothy is central to our walk with **God**. The Apostle Paul's emphasis on passing down spiritual teachings to "faithful men" underlines the quintessence of faithfulness in our Christian journey.

In our fast-paced world, it is often easy to misconstrue or transpose the true intent of the scriptures. Just as there can be errors in simple human tasks, such as typing a letter 'A' as 'E', so too can we inadvertently misinterpret the Word of **God**. Notably, we've mistakenly promoted practices like isolation when we should be preaching separation, or conflated humility with inferiority. Yet, these concepts are not synonymous.

"For God hath not given us the spirit of fear; but of power, and of love, and of a sound mind." - 2 Timothy 1:7 (KJV)

When the scripture emphasizes the importance of committing to faithful men, it is highlighting a fundamental principle in **God's** kingdom. **God's** commitment isn't anchored in our humanly perceived talents, but rather in our character. Our talents, as meritorious as they might seem, are a product of human efforts. On the contrary, our character reflects **God's** transformative work in us.

Abraham, a paragon of faith, is an exemplary figure in this discourse. Everywhere he journeyed, Abraham built an altar to the **Lord**, signifying his unwavering faith and commitment. In contrast, he merely pitched his tent, indicating the temporary nature of our earthly sojourn.

"And he removed from thence unto a mountain on the east of Bethel, and pitched his tent, having Bethel on the west, and Hai on the east: and there he builded an altar unto the LORD, and called upon the name of the LORD." - Genesis 12:8 (KJV)

Today, there is a profound inversion of this practice. Many have chosen to establish their earthly tents, placing undue emphasis on temporal accomplishments while neglecting the eternal altars of spiritual commitment and faithfulness to **God**.

Character, as illuminated by faithfulness, is the bedrock of our relationship with **God**. **God's** unchanging nature and **His** unwavering faithfulness to us are what secure our trust in **Him.** Equally, our faithfulness to **God** and **His** word establishes our relationship with **Him,** setting the path for us to be instruments in **His** divine plan.

In , while the world may champion talents and charisma, in the eyes of **God**, faithfulness remains paramount. **God's Mighty Men** are not just those endowed with talents but those who, in their heart of hearts, remain faithful and committed to **His** cause. As we navigate our

Christian journey, may we strive to be among those faithful men, upon whom **God** can rely to teach and guide others in **His** ways.

Harnessing Faithfulness & Unity for Kingdom Power

#1. Faithful

"All you've got to have is faithfulness and **God** will give you the ability. You don't have to pray for ability. This statement encapsulates the essence of **God's** desire for **His** people. The Bible is rich with examples of ordinary individuals who, by simply being faithful, were equipped by **God** to carry out great feats.

"It is required in stewards, that a man be found faithful." (1 Corinthians 4:2 KJV)

God doesn't necessarily look for the strongest, the smartest, or the most capable. **He looks for the faithful.** When **God** finds someone committed to **Him, He** equips that individual with all they need to fulfill **His** purpose.

"But the fruit of the Spirit is love, joy, peace, longsuffering, gentleness, goodness, faith," (Galatians 5:22 KJV)

#2. Communication

One of the foundational truths highlighted is the importance of communication. The scripture says, **"So then faith cometh by hearing, and hearing by the**

word of God." (Romans 10:17 KJV). Communication is the basis of life, and through it, **God's** word is spread, faith is ignited, and hearts are transformed.

#3. Giving and Receiving
Next, exchange is highlighted as the process of life. **God's** kingdom operates on the principle of giving and receiving. **Jesus** said, **"Give, and it shall be given unto you; good measure, pressed down, and shaken together, and running over, shall men give into your bosom." (Luke 6:38 KJV)**

#4. Balance
The fourth truth is about balance, which is the key to life. Solomon, in his wisdom, acknowledged the need for balance, **"To every thing there is a season, and a time to every purpose under the heaven:" (Ecclesiastes 3:1 KJV)**

#5. Agreement
Lastly, agreement, termed as the power of life, holds immense significance. **Jesus** emphasized this saying, **"Again I say unto you, That if two of you shall agree on earth as touching any thing that they shall ask, it shall be done for them of my Father which is in heaven." (Matthew 18:19 KJV).** The power of unity and agreement can never be underestimated, especially in the realm of faith.

In talking to fathers, one realizes the importance of unity in the family setup. It is crucial that fathers understand their role in bringing unity, for it is through unity that power is released in the family. Scripture emphasizes the blessings of unity: **"Behold, how good and how pleasant it is for brethren to dwell together in unity!" (Psalms 133:1 KJV)**

In the tapestry of faith, faithfulness stands out as the golden thread. It is through unwavering commitment to **God** that we unlock the potential **He** has placed within us. As **Mighty Men** and women in **Christ**, embracing the foundational truths of communication, exchange, balance, and agreement can transform our lives and impact the kingdom of **God**. Through unity, the power of the kingdom is made manifest, creating ripples of change in our world. Let us therefore commit to being faithful stewards, harnessing the power of agreement, and walking in the balance **God** has set for us, illuminating **His Mighty** power in our lives.

.

CHAPTER FIVE

Authority, Agreement, and Accountability in the Light of Scripture

In every familial structure, unity and agreement lay the groundwork for a harmonious environment. An ancient piece of wisdom states, **"Never, ever disagree with your wife in front of your children because to the degree that you disagree with your wife in front of your children, you lose authority over them."** This understanding underlines the significance of unity. As it is stated, "The place of agreement is the place of power." Unity and accord bring strength, while division and strife bring weakness. We find a supporting scripture in the Bible where the Apostle Paul speaks to the church in Philippi, urging them towards unity:

"Fulfil ye my joy, that ye be likeminded, having the same love, being of one accord, of one mind." (Philippians 2:2, KJV)

Powerlessness often stems from disagreements. This concept isn't novel. When parents present a fractured front, children can exploit these divisions. This exploitation of divisions can be traced back to the hippie generation, where disillusionment and rebellion against authority rose from observing consistent disunity in their households.

A key principle in the understanding of authority is the realization that true authority isn't just about wielding power but is rooted deeply in responsibility and accountability. This thought leads us to a reflective observation of the current state of manhood. For a significant duration, society has endured the era of the mediocre man. These are the men who yearn for authority's privileges but shy away from the responsibilities that come with it. However, there is hope on the horizon. **"We're coming out of the era of the mediocre man."** The Body of **Christ**, as well as the world need to witnessing an awakening among men to higher ideals and greater responsibility.

The Bible is replete with examples and teachings on authority and accountability. We are reminded of the Parable of the Talents in the book of Matthew, where servants are given varying amounts of talents, and upon the master's return, are held accountable for how they managed them. The servant who failed to utilize his talent faced severe consequences. As stated, **"For unto every one that hath shall be given, and he shall have abundance: but from him that hath not shall be taken away even that which he hath." (Matthew 25:29, KJV)**

In every home, there are men seeking the authority that comes with their roles as husbands, fathers, and household leaders. But the truest essence of that authority lies in the willingness to be accountable. "**God** never gives authority without accountability."

In , to build strong families and communities, one must prioritize unity, embrace the responsibilities of authority, and be accountable for one's actions. The scriptures provide the wisdom and guidance needed for this endeavor, urging us towards unity and righteousness. As men, and indeed as believers, may we rise to this call, understanding that authority and accountability go hand in hand in **God's** divine design.

The Balance of Authority and Accountability

One profound and overarching truth that resonates across all walks of life, be it in politics, society, or spirituality, is the balance between authority and accountability. In analyzing the dynamics of authority, one can draw parallels from various facets of life to bring out its significance in the light of scriptures.

Consider, for instance, the workings of our Congress. Many seek authority, yet shy away from the consequential weight of accountability. A chorus of amens often punctuates such observations, nodding to a shared acknowledgment of this human tendency. Yet, this attitude isn't confined to the political arena alone. Even in the realm of Christianity, this same struggle manifests. Across the country, myriad prayer groups emerge, a testament to the multitude that seeks spiritual authority. Yet, they often resist formal affiliations and memberships – structures that might hold them accountable.

However, the teachings of **Jesus Christ**, encapsulated in **His** parables, provide a blueprint on this matter. The parable of the pounds and talents drives home the message that **God** does not hand out authority without tethering it to accountability.

"For the kingdom of heaven is as a man travelling into a far country, who called his own servants, and delivered unto them his goods. And unto one he gave five talents, to another two, and to another one; to every man according to his several ability; and straightway took his journey." – Matthew 25:14-15 KJV

Within the context of relationships, particularly marriage, the tension between seeking authority and dodging accountability is palpable. Often, when a man seeks dominion without acknowledging his actions or lapses – and his wife yearns for him to be accountable – he misconstrues her intent as nagging. Yet, beneath these mundane altercations lies the eternal principle of spiritual accountability.

"God never gives authority without accountability."

It is a creed that every believer should internalize. Our relationship with **God**, akin to our connections within the family, church, and society, is anchored in accountability. As stewards of **God's** grace and blessings, every individual will be called to account, if not today, then in the afterlife.

In the Gospel of John, the scripture affirms the spiritual authority vested in believers:

"But as many as received him, to them gave he power to become the sons of God, even to them that believe on his name." – John 1:12 KJV

To pose a reflective question: How many of us have truly embraced our rebirth in **Christ**? And having received the authority to become children of **God**, are we prepared for the inevitable accountability that accompanies it?

The journey of a believer is one of navigating the twin pillars of authority and accountability. Authority without accountability is an imbalance, a recipe for chaos. Drawing insights from the scriptures and the teachings of **Jesus Christ**, it becomes evident that **God**, in **His** infinite wisdom, always couples authority with accountability. As recipients of **His** divine grace and authority, it is our sacred duty to uphold and cherish the responsibility that comes with it, affirming our steadfast commitment to **His** eternal principles.

Stewardship and the Anointing of the Holy Spirit

"Let a man so account of us, as of the ministers of Christ, and stewards of the mysteries of God. Moreover it is required in stewards, that a man be found faithful." (1 Corinthians 4:1-2 KJV)

In our daily walk with the **Lord**, there is a profound

responsibility placed upon each of us. This responsibility transcends the occasional recognition or acknowledgment; it's a deep-seated accountability that **God** demands from us every single day. Paul, in his letter to the Corinthians, emphasized the importance of stewardship, noting that we are stewards of the mysteries of **God**.

Our understanding of stewardship, as it often happens, is limited to the management of our finances. But **God's** perspective on stewardship encompasses more than monetary assets. It includes the gift of time, the talent we possess, and the message of the gospel that we've received. In the words of the Apostle Peter: "As every man hath received the gift, even so minister the same one to another, as good stewards of the manifold grace of **God**." (1 Peter 4:10 KJV)

However, a pitfall exists that some churches and believers fall into. They gather and bask in the presence of the Holy Spirit, taking in the anointing, feeling edified, and uplifted. Yet, they forget a crucial aspect of this anointing. The Holy Spirit is not just for personal edification. As Paul writes in the letter to the Ephesians: "Unto me, who am less than the least of all saints, is this grace given, that I should preach among the Gentiles the unsearchable riches of **Christ**;" (Ephesians 3:8 KJV). The anointing we receive is not just for us to be blessed but to be a blessing unto others. It's to equip us to proclaim the unsearchable riches of **Jesus Christ**.

If we continuously partake in this anointing without directing it towards ministering to others, we risk being like the servant in **Jesus**'s parable who buried his talent instead of multiplying it. "But he that had received one went and digged in the earth, and hid his lord's money." (Matthew 25:18 KJV) We must always be wary of becoming spiritually selfish, where we relish in the Holy Spirit's edification but fail to extend its blessings to others.

In, **God's Mighty Men** are not just receivers of **His** grace and anointing but are active stewards, using these gifts to further the kingdom of **God**. True stewardship involves recognizing the breadth of our responsibility, from our time, talents, finances, to the gospel and anointing we've been gifted. It's an ever-present reminder that **God's** gifts, while meant to bless us, are also intended to flow through us to bless others. As believers, let us strive to be good stewards of the manifold grace of **God**, ensuring that we don't merely store the treasures we've been given but actively share them with the world around us.

An Exploration of God's Mighty Men in the Scriptures

Everyone has a purpose in life. As we navigate our existence, it is crucial to recognize that **God** holds us accountable for the gifts and talents he has endowed us with. Notably, the Holy Spirit anoints us, and this anointing comes with a responsibility.

"For unto whomsoever much is given, of him shall be much required: and to whom men have committed much, of him they will ask the more." (Luke 12:48, KJV)

This sentiment of accountability is further echoed in Luke 13 through the Parable of the Fig Tree. In this parable, a barren fig tree is given one more year to bear fruit, with the gardener promising to nurture it. If it still does not bear fruit after that time, it will be cut down.

"**He** spake also this parable; A certain man had a fig tree planted in his vineyard; and he came and sought fruit thereon and found none. Then said he unto the dresser of his vineyard, Behold, these three years I come seeking fruit on this fig tree, and find none: cut it down; why cumbereth it the ground?" (Luke 13:6-7, KJV)

Drawing parallels from this, what is the fruit that **God** expects from us? Nature teaches us that everything yields according to its kind. Just as you wouldn't expect oranges from an apple tree or eagles from quail, our spiritual lives should bear the fruits **God** has designed us to produce.

Our purpose isn't just about what we accomplish materially or the accolades we gather. In essence, it is about reaching the pinnacle of our spiritual and moral potential - manhood in **Christ**. Without **Jesus**, we fall short, as Paul reminds us:

"For all have sinned, and come short of the glory of God;" (Romans 3:23, KJV)

But with **Christ**, we are called to a higher purpose and standard. Through **Him,** our manhood is epitimized, our potential is unlocked, and our purpose is clear.

"I can do all things through Christ which strengtheneth me." (Philippians 4:13, KJV)

So, as we gather today, let us remember our mission: to bear the fruit **God** has intended for us and to walk in the fullness of the manhood **He** desires for us. This is not just a lesson, but a clarion call to step up, to rise, and to embrace the fullness of **God's Mighty** purpose for us.

God's desire for us is clear: to epitomize our manhood in **Him.** By understanding our purpose and bearing the fruits **God** expects of us, we step into our role as **God's Mighty Men**. As the scriptures affirm, when much is given, much is expected. Let's heed this call and rise to the occasion, fulfilling our divine mandate and shining as lights in this world. Amen.

A Call to Authentic Transformation

It has been said that the core of understanding is more profound when rooted in shared experiences. This truth is foundational to the concept that in every corner of the globe, despite our cultural, societal, or religious differences, we are bound together by our shared humanity. The journey to discovering our **God**-given potential is universal, an exploration that leads to transformation, guided by **His** word and principles. This teaching seeks to unpack the importance of genuine change from a biblical perspective, emphasizing the significance of discerning intention from action.

"For as the body without the spirit is dead, so faith without works is dead also." - James 2:26 KJV

We often hear exhortations, pleas, and passionate sermons calling for change in our lives. Yet, the emphasis here is not on the outward display of fervor or religious emotion, but on genuine transformation. In **God's** eyes, the fruit of our labor speaks louder than our intentions. A shout or proclamation, though passionate, is ephemeral. But a life transformed by **His** word is a testimony that resounds through eternity.

"But be ye doers of the word, and not hearers only, deceiving your own selves." - James 1:22 KJV

A common pitfall in human nature is our tendency to judge others solely based on their actions while extending grace to ourselves based on our intentions. This skewed judgment is rooted in our limited perspective, seeing only the external actions of others, while intimately aware of our inner thoughts and motivations. However, this mindset stands contrary to **God's** teachings. **He** calls us to a higher standard, to look beyond ourselves and our biases.

"Judge not, that ye be not judged. For with what judgment ye judge, ye shall be judged: and with what measure ye mete, it shall be measured to you again." - Matthew 7:1-2 KJV

While traveling in Southeast Asia, the uniformity of human nature became starkly evident. Regardless of whether one is in Philippines or America, certain truths remain unchanged. No matter our status – CEO or commoner, there's a fundamental commonality. We all, metaphorically, "put our pants on one leg at a time." This speaks volumes about the universal need for the word of **God**. It transcends boundaries, speaking to the heart of every man.

"For there is no respect of persons with God." - Romans 2:11 KJV

As we journey through life, seeking transformation and alignment with **God's** purpose, we are reminded of the significance of genuine change. The challenge is to bridge the gap between our intentions and our actions. **God's Mighty Men** are not defined by the robes they wear, the titles they hold, or the regions they hail from. They are defined by their transformed lives, their dedication to the word, and their commitment to embody the principles of the scriptures. Let us strive not for mere reactions but for results in our spiritual journey, results that manifest in lives truly changed by **God's** word.

"Therefore if any man be in Christ, he is a new creature: old things are passed away; behold, all things are become new." - 2 Corinthians 5:17 KJV

Unity in the Blood of Christ

Throughout the ages and across different cultures, one fundamental truth remains constant: human experiences are, at their core, common to all men. This truth surpasses cultural, racial, and societal boundaries. Despite these variations, deep down, everyone is simply a human being, created by **God**. One might even argue that the essence of human existence transcends the superficial differences that we often prioritize, such as skin color or cultural background. As the Bible says, **"And hath made of one blood all nations of men for to dwell on all the face of the earth" (Acts 17:26 KJV).**

The kingdom of **God** operates in stark contrast to worldly systems. In **God's** kingdom, external appearances or backgrounds don't define an individual's worth or significance. Rather, it is the blood that flows within our veins – a poignant reminder that we all come from one source. More importantly, as Christians, we believe in the redemptive power of one specific blood – that of **Jesus Christ**. This belief unites us all, making us brethren regardless of our earthly distinctions. **"But now in Christ Jesus ye who sometimes were far off are made nigh by the blood of Christ" (Ephesians 2:13 KJV).**

However, humans, in their flawed nature, have a recurring problem: the proclivity to judge others based on their actions while evaluating themselves based on intentions. It's a common human trait, one that everyone can resonate with, whether they admit it or not. As mentioned in **Matthew 7:3 KJV, "And why beholdest**

thou the mote that is in thy brother's eye, but considerest not the beam that is in thine own eye?"

Turning our attention to 1 Corinthians 10, we find invaluable teachings that provide a blueprint for Christian living. But even before delving into this, it's important to recognize the pivotal role of **God's** Word in transforming lives. As mentioned in **Psalm 107:20 KJV: "He sent his word, and healed them, and delivered them from their destructions."** This passage underscores the transformative and restorative power of **God's** Word. It doesn't merely instruct; it heals, redeems, and delivers.

In the end, **God's** message, as reflected in the scriptures, is clear: humans are unified not by externalities but by the blood of **Christ**, which offers redemption and transformation. By recognizing the inherent unity of all humanity and the transformative power of **God's** Word, Christians everywhere can transcend earthly divisions and foster a spirit of unity, acceptance, and love. After all, as the body of **Christ**, it is our duty to reflect **His** teachings and **His** love to the world.

Patterns, Principles, and Pursuit of Excellence

"He sent his word, and healed them, and delivered them from their destructions." - Psalm 107:20 (KJV)

God is characterized by consistency, pattern, and principle. In every stroke of **His** work, there lies a detailed blueprint that demonstrates **His** excellence. **He**

has orchestrated the universe with intentionality and precision, always working based on patterns and principles. If we can discern and adhere to these patterns and principles in the scriptures, we unlock the keys to **His** kingdom and are destined for success.

God's word, as conveyed in Psalm 107:20, is not only for healing but also for deliverance. It is a testament to **His** unwavering desire to bring restoration and redemption to **His** people.

The tragedy, however, is that many fall short of tapping into this excellence. They settle for 'good,' letting it be the adversary of the 'best'. This mediocrity arises when we adopt the life patterns designed by others for us. It's like trying to fit a square peg into a round hole. Without discovering and fitting into **God's** unique pattern for our lives, true fulfillment remains elusive.

"For my thoughts are not your thoughts, neither are your ways my ways, saith the Lord." - Isaiah 55:8 (KJV)

Pastors, businessmen, leaders, and every individual must heed this truth. Many leaders often falter because they become ensnared by the philosophies of men. Such philosophies are, many times, mere rationalizations that mask failure. When we adopt such reasoning, we inadvertently inherit their failures.

God's uniqueness in creation is evident. While humans have common features, every person is a distinct masterpiece, a reflection of **God's** love for individuality.

It's this individuality, this unique pattern crafted by **God**, that we must discover and align with to achieve success in our endeavors, be it in ministry, business, marriage, or any other aspect of life.

In Matthew 25, we read the Parable of the Talents, a depiction of how different individuals handle what's entrusted to them by **God**.

"For the kingdom of heaven is as a man travelling into a far country, who called his own servants, and delivered unto them his goods." - Matthew 25:14 (KJV)

This parable reveals a vital lesson: actions speak louder than words. The servant who did the least also made the most excuses. It's a sobering reminder that justifications and excuses can never replace genuine results.

As believers, our quest should be to unearth and align with the unique pattern **God** has set for our lives. This journey requires moving beyond worldly philosophies and rationalizations, and deeply immersing ourselves in the principles of the Word. When we live according to **God's** patterns and principles, we not only experience success but also fulfill the divine purpose **He** has for us. Excuses might offer temporary solace, but genuine accomplishment comes only from working in line with **God's** plan. In this journey of faith, let's remember: excuses are not reasons. Instead, let's aim for the excellence **God** has destined for us, as **His Mighty Men** and women. Amen.

The Power of Positivity in Faith

"O give thanks unto the LORD; for he is good: for his mercy endureth forever." - Psalm 136:1 (KJV)

The essence of faith, as understood through the scriptures, is an unwavering trust in the divine plan and purpose of **God**. We find ourselves at times offering excuses for our hesitations, our doubts, and our failures. Envisage standing before the throne of **God**, faced with the daunting question of how one has lived in the light of **His** Son, **Jesus Christ**.

"Every way of a man is right in his own eyes: but the LORD pondereth the hearts." - Proverbs 21:2 (KJV)

It is quite effortless to fall into the trap of justifying our actions with trivial reasons. Perhaps, it was an unpleasant experience at church, or maybe the challenges of life made the path of faith seem burdensome. These excuses, when weighed against the grandeur of **God's** purpose, seem trivial. It begs the question: why do we often find reasons to drift from the path **God** has set for us?

"Let us not be weary in well doing: for in due season we shall reap, if we faint not." - Galatians 6:9 (KJV)

One of the profound truths, as highlighted in the divine promise that **God** does not envisage failure for those who place their trust in **Him.** From the stories of Genesis to the prophetic words in Revelation, there's a resounding theme that rings true: **God** never predestined failure for those who put their trust in **Him.**

"For I know the plans I have for you, declares the LORD, plans for welfare and not for evil, to give you a future and a hope." - Jeremiah 29:11 (KJV)

This principle emphasizes the underlying positivity that underscores **God's** plan. The divine blueprint isn't built upon negativity but thrives on positivity. When **God** seeks to create, nurture, or change, **He** does so on the foundation of positivity. This is the very reason that confession and repentance are crucial; they allow us to shed the negative and embrace the positive.

"Let everything that hath breath praise the LORD. Praise ye the LORD." - Psalm 150:6 (KJV)

Our relationship with the divine is nurtured not in complaints, grievances, or criticisms but in praises. **God** doesn't inhabit the negative. **He** thrives in the praises of **His** people. For praise, at its core, is the affirmation of positivity, the acknowledgment of **His** goodness, and the reflection of our faith.

In , the call to each believer is clear. To tread the path of faith with unwavering positivity, trusting in **God's** plan, and enveloping our lives in praises. For in doing so, we align ourselves with the divine blueprint, embracing the blessings and promises that **God** has in store.

"And whatsoever ye do, do it heartily, as to the Lord, and not unto men." - Colossians 3:23 (KJV)

Embracing the Power of Resurrection

"But the hour cometh, and now is, when the true worshippers shall worship the Father in spirit and in truth: for the Father seeketh such to worship him." - John 4:23 (KJV)

When we speak of **God's** praise, we delve into the very heart of appreciation, gratitude, and adoration. Praise, in its essence, stands as a testament to the goodness and grandeur of **God**. It resonates in the positive, echoing our heartfelt thanks and reverent admiration for the Almighty. On the contrary, flattery, as elucidated in the Proverbs, skews towards the negative, often serving as veiled hostility.

"A man that flattereth his neighbour spreadeth a net for his feet." - Proverbs 29:5 (KJV)

Many are quick to show appreciation for teachings that bring comfort and solace. However, the true essence of **God's** word is not just to provide solace, but to challenge, convict, and transform. The teachings of men like Juan Carlos Ortiz exemplify this. **God's** word is designed to be a mirror, reflecting our imperfections, pushing us towards transformation. For it is in acknowledging our imperfections that we find the path to true transformation.

"For whom he did foreknow, he also did predestinate to be conformed to the image of his Son, that he might be the firstborn among many brethren." - Romans

8:29 (KJV)

The crucifixion and resurrection of **Jesus Christ** serve as a profound analogy for our spiritual journey. **God** doesn't call us just to identify with the crucifixion - the death to our sins and worldly desires - but more crucially, to embrace the resurrection. The act of baptism represents this beautifully. It's not about staying submerged in the waters of our old self but rising renewed, embodying the resurrected life.

"I am crucified with Christ: nevertheless I live; yet not I, but Christ liveth in me: and the life which I now live in the flesh I live by the faith of the Son of God, who loved me, and gave himself for me." - Galatians 2:20 (KJV)

In, the call for **God's Mighty Men** is a journey from mere appreciation to transformative faith. It's about moving beyond fleeting moments of spiritual euphoria to a sustained life of resurrection power. Embracing this journey means living not in the shadow of the crucifixion but in the radiant light of the resurrection, where true power and purpose are found.

"That I may know him, and the power of his resurrection, and the fellowship of his sufferings, being made conformable unto his death." - Philippians 3:10 (KJV)

Living Above the Circumstances

In a world that constantly emphasizes the challenges we face, it's important to recognize the power that comes from living in the resurrection. As Christians, we're reminded in **Romans 6:4, "Therefore we are buried with him by baptism into death: that like as Christ was raised up from the dead by the glory of the Father, even so we also should walk in newness of life."** It is this newness of life that empowers us to rise above our circumstances.

Many people claim to be "doing pretty good under the circumstances." However, a life lived under circumstances is not the life of the resurrected. True, challenges, like rain, may come and sometimes persist, causing areas of our lives to feel gloomy. But in **Christ**, we do not remain under this gloom. As the adage humorously yet insightfully suggests, even when it is raining cats and dogs, there's a sunny sky above those clouds. To emphasize this**, Psalms 113:3** says, **"From the rising of the sun unto the going down of the same the Lord's name is to be praised."**

In the throes of our trials, our faith in **God** encourages us to declare that "Above the clouds, the sun always shines." This repeated proclamation is not just a statement of fact but a declaration of faith, hope, and optimism.

One of the most profound revelations is the assurance that **God** doesn't conclude things on a negative note. No matter the trials, tribulations, and adversities, **He** ensures a favorable end for those who trust in **Him. Romans 8:28** reassures us, **"And we know that all things work together for good to them that love God, to them who are the called according to his purpose."**

There are prophecies and there are fears surrounding the end times. The discussions about the antichrist, the mark of the beast, and the looming global challenges can be overwhelming. Yet, these aren't the final chapters of our story. The Word reminds us in **2 Peter 3:10, "But the day of the Lord will come as a thief in the night; in the which the heavens shall pass away with a great noise, and the elements shall melt with fervent heat, the earth also and the works that are therein shall be burned up."** Beyond this, we have the hope of a new Earth, an Earth purified and ready for the saints.

God's intention is always for a brighter and better end. **He** has designed a future where the redeemed will inherit the Earth in its purest form. Every trial, tribulation, and seeming setback is but a temporary moment before the unveiling of **God's** ultimate purpose.

In our journey of faith, let us take inspiration from the **Mighty Men** and women of **God** who lived their lives with the unwavering belief that the sun always shines above the clouds. Our **God** is a positive **God**, and **He** ensures that every story committed to Him shifts from the negative to the positive. In moments of doubt, let's remember the promise in **Jeremiah 29:11, "For I know the thoughts that I think toward you, saith the Lord, thoughts of peace, and not of evil, to give you an**

expected end." God's Mighty Men and Women are those who live above their circumstances, holding onto **God's** promises, and expecting a glorious end.

The Power of Grace and Glory

The essence of humanity's relationship with the divine is grounded in trust and commitment. When one fathoms the profundity of **God's** magnanimity, it becomes evident that **His** divine plan is not geared towards letting **His** faithful end in negativity. Our allegiance, our commitments, and our prayers are quintessential in shaping this bond. As it is written, **"And we know that all things work together for good to them that love God, to them who are the called according to his purpose" (Romans 8:28 KJV).**

Prayer is not a mere ritual or an act to be performed in compulsion. The motivation to pray should not be external validations or the dictates of societal norms. Instead, it should be an intrinsic yearning, a spontaneous outpouring of one's heart, and an act of love towards the Creator. The Apostle Paul tells us, **"Pray without ceasing" (1 Thessalonians 5:17 KJV)**, emphasizing the ceaseless communion with **God** that should be an intrinsic part of our existence.

There's an innate tendency in humanity to be lawbreakers. When guided by our carnal natures, we often fall prey to making vows only to break them later. This phenomenon can be observed universally among believers and non-believers alike. The act of setting a personal law, be it committing to daily Bible reading or fixed prayer hours, often leads to its violation. As the scripture rightly points out, **"For all have sinned, and come short of the glory of God;" (Romans 3:23 KJV),** highlighting our inherent imperfect nature.

However, it is crucial to understand that our spiritual endeavors are not meant to be dictated by laws but by grace. **"For by grace are ye saved through faith; and that not of yourselves: it is the gift of God: Not of works, lest any man should boast" (Ephesians 2:8-9 KJV).** Grace, an unmerited favor from **God**, is the balm that heals our sins. When we embrace this grace, we transition from being mere sinners to saints, bathed in **God's** glory.

Biblical words remind us of the dual nature of **God's** benevolence: grace for sinners and glory for saints. The grace of **God** is a protective shield, guarding us in our vulnerable moments of sin. However, beyond grace lies the realm of glory—a state where we are immersed in righteousness and filled with **God's** majesty. **"But we all, with open face beholding as in a glass the glory of the Lord, are changed into the same image from glory to glory, even as by the Spirit of the Lord" (2 Corinthians 3:18 KJV).**

In essence, while grace is essential for our spiritual survival, glory should be our aspiration. To limit oneself to seeking **God's** grace is to remain content with spiritual infancy. To truly thrive and flourish in the Kingdom of **God**, one must ardently pursue the glory that comes from living a life in resonance with **His** divine will.

The journey of **God's Mighty Men** is a testament to the power of grace and the pursuit of glory. It's a reminder that in the ebb and flow of life, while our imperfections might make us stumble, **God's** grace is ever-present. However, the ultimate fulfillment lies not just in receiving this grace but in transcending it to bask in the radiant glory of **God**. This glory is not just an external reward but an internal transformation that aligns us with **God's** purpose, propelling us forward in our spiritual journey.

Seeking Glory in Divine Purpose

"For all have sinned, and come short of the glory of God." - Romans 3:23 (KJV)

The call to embrace the divine glory is a journey of both personal transformation and collective revival. It is an invitation to rise above the mundane, the limited, and the temporal, and be filled with the magnificence of **God's** presence. It is in this seeking that the foundation of manhood is built, with unwavering faith and unyielding commitment.

"And let them offer sacrifices of thanksgiving, and declare his works with rejoicing." - Psalm 107:22 (KJV)

Every gathering of believers is a testament to the presence of **God's** glory. This is evident in the passion with which worship is raised, hands lifted, and hearts surrendered. The **Mighty Men** and women of **God** do not merely sit as spectators; they actively engage in the worship experience, boldly declaring, "Fill me with your glory, **Lord**!" Such a plea is a reflection of an understanding of **God's** redemptive grace – grace that forgives, heals, and restores.

"And the Word was made flesh, and dwelt among us, (and we beheld his glory, the glory as of the only begotten of the Father,) full of grace and truth." - John 1:14 (KJV)

This fervent prayer is not just a request for a fleeting experience but a deep yearning for a sustained transformation. For in **God's** glory, there is strength, upliftment, and power. The glory of **God** fills our heart, soul, and spirit, leading us to a profound experience that transcends the natural.

In gatherings, the church becomes a conduit of **God's** glory, channeling **His** divine power and grace to every participant. But such glory is not reserved for the confines of the church alone. **God's Mighty Men** carry this glory everywhere they go, illuminating their path, reflecting the divine, and influencing their world.

"He sent his word, and healed them, and delivered them from their destructions." - Psalm 107:20 (KJV)

The pathway to manhood is anchored in understanding the patterns and principles of **God**. Everything **God** does is orchestrated with precision, order, and purpose. While it's essential to remember these patterns, the manifestations of **God's** glory are also evident in miraculous ways. Miracles that confound human logic and reveal the limitless expanse of divine intervention.

In, **God's Mighty Men** are not marked by their physical strength or worldly accomplishments but by their relentless pursuit of **God's** glory. They recognize the importance of divine patterns and principles and are always ready to witness the miraculous, ever so eager to declare, "Hallelujah, fill us with your glory today, **Lord**!". The journey to becoming one of **God's Mighty Men** starts with a sincere heart, ready to be filled with **His** glory, and a life lived in adherence to **His** word.

"To the chief Musician, A Psalm of David. The heavens declare the glory of God; and the firmament sheweth his handywork." - Psalm 19:1 (KJV)

The Pattern of Divine Revelation and Love in the Church

"The apostles spoke in tongues, illustrating the power of **God** in inexplicable ways. As written in the book of Acts, **"And they were all filled with the Holy Ghost, and began to speak with other tongues, as the Spirit gave them utterance." (Acts 2:4, KJV).**

The unequivocal head of the church is **Jesus Christ**. Repeated emphasis, "**Jesus** is the head of the church," draws from the book of Colossians, where Paul writes, **"And he is the head of the body, the church: who is the beginning, the firstborn from the dead; that in all things he might have the preeminence." (Colossians 1:18, KJV).**

God's pattern of operation is notably unique and consistent. **He** speaks forth a word, which in turn incarnates into a body that brings healing to the world. The prime and unparalleled example of this pattern is when the Word became flesh in the person of **Jesus**. As it is written, **"And the Word was made flesh, and dwelt among us, (and we beheld his glory, the glory as of the only begotten of the Father,) full of grace and truth." (John 1:14, KJV).**

When **God** communicates, it isn't merely informational but revelational. Every divine message carries a transformative power. The process of receiving **God's** word is marked by revelation, which transitions into inspiration. Through this inspiration, profound internal changes occur: **"Therefore if any man be in Christ, he is a new creature: old things are passed away; behold, all things are become new." (2 Corinthians 5:17, KJV).**

A changed heart becomes a reservoir of divine love, manifesting externally as love for fellow believers. This love isn't merely human affection but a divine mandate. The Apostle John wrote, **"If a man say, I love God, and**

hateth his brother, he is a liar: for he that loveth not his brother whom he hath seen, how can he love God whom he hath not seen?" (1 John 4:20, KJV).

In, **God's Mighty Men** are those who recognize the pattern of **God's** working, embrace the transformative power of **His** word, and manifest the love of **God** in their relationships within the church. This love, an evidence of divine regeneration, is a testament to the indwelling of **God's** Spirit. It is imperative, therefore, that as believers, we understand the importance of not just receiving **God's** word but also embodying it in love towards our brethren, chosen by **God** Himself.

CHAPTER SIX

God's Mighty Men and Their Journey Through Faith

The tapestry of life is a confluence of spiritual progressions and tangible experiences. Central to this journey is the guiding light of faith, the unwavering belief that binds humanity with divinity. At the heart of this spiritual odyssey are **God's Mighty Men**, figures of exceptional conviction and resolve, propelled by divine inspirations and guided by the Holy Word. The following discourse seeks to unravel the nuances of spiritual maturity, drawing from the teachings of the Bible, and emphasizing the significance of transitions in our spiritual lives.

When divine inspiration strikes the soul, it demands formalization. Such a transformative experience impels us to align ourselves with like-minded souls, those who harbor "precious faith like precious faith." The journey towards spiritual maturity, as the body of **Christ** perceives it, is not a stagnant one. As is elucidated in **1 Peter 1:5-7:**

"Who are kept by the power of God through faith unto salvation ready to be revealed in the last time. Wherein ye greatly rejoice, though now for a season, if need be, ye are in heaviness through manifold temptations: That the trial of your faith, being much

more precious than of gold that perisheth, though it be tried with fire, might be found unto praise and honour and glory at the appearing of Jesus Christ:"

This scripture delineates the path of maturation in faith. As we grow in grace and strengthen our bond with the Almighty, our interpersonal relationships too undergo metamorphoses. Not all tread the path of faith with the same fervor and conviction. The dynamics of faith are complex. A friend who does not progress with you in faith can unknowingly stifle your own growth. Aligning with those of "precious faith" thus becomes paramount. This alignment ensures that we are ever receptive to **God's** grand design for us.

In delineating the kingdom principles, **Jesus** highlighted two fundamental actions that dictate our lives - entering and leaving. The cyclical nature of these actions can be seen in our mundane routines. As we transition from one space to another, from the bedroom to the bathroom, and further to the kitchen and beyond, we embody these kingdom principles. Our relationships too, are governed by these very principles.

But the essence of spiritual growth is not limited to mere physical transitions. Divine interventions often lead us to forge bonds and partake in ministries. But just as the heavens planned our entry into these divine pursuits, the exit, often grounded in our worldly realm, appears deceptively mundane. It is, however, crucial to realize that **God's** workings, though sometimes inconspicuous, are omnipresent. The evidence of **His** hand in our lives is omnipresent, be it in the grandeur of a divine revelation or the subtlety of a natural transition.

Life is punctuated with crises. Each phase, from the safety of the womb to the trials of adolescence, presents its own set of challenges. But, as evident in **Romans 5:3-5:**

"And not only so, but we glory in tribulations also: knowing that tribulation worketh patience; And patience, experience; and experience, hope: And hope maketh not ashamed; because the love of God is shed abroad in our hearts by the Holy Ghost which is given unto us."

Crises, thus, are not mere roadblocks; they are essential catalysts for growth.

The path of spiritual maturity, adorned with the guidance of **God's Mighty Men** and the sacred scriptures, is a journey through faith, transitions, and personal growth. As we tread this path, it is crucial to remember that every challenge and every transition is a testament to **God's** divine plan. In aligning with those of precious faith and understanding the intrinsic value of both entering and leaving, we embrace the fullness of our spiritual journey, drawing closer to the Almighty with each step.

Embracing Crisis and Seeking

Growth Through Divine Intervention

In contemporary times, society has become a hub of individuals chasing after the elusive concept of perpetual happiness. Many perceive crises as unwarranted deviations from a serene path, a belief perhaps stemming from the pervasive happiness culture that surrounds us. However, examining scriptural and historical references, we observe that crises are not only pivotal but also divinely ordained moments that are intrinsic to growth and spiritual maturation.

The life of Joseph, as portrayed in the Bible, is a testament to this. When Joseph was betrayed by his brothers, sold into slavery, and falsely imprisoned, these were not random events, but rather orchestrated divine intersections for his ultimate elevation. **His** life's narrative succinctly captures this essence: **"But as for you, ye thought evil against me; but God meant it unto good, to bring to pass, as it is this day, to save much people alive." (Genesis 50:20, KJV)**. This verse illustrates how **God** can turn what appears to be a crisis into an opportunity for growth and fulfillment of **His** purpose.

A crisis is a requisite path from the transitory to the enduring. Consider marital relationships. Crises, no matter how trivial, like disagreements over household chores or deeper conflicts, are instrumental in refining the bond between spouses. It is through these trials that relationships solidify and mature.

Entrepreneurs and business owners will testify that with

growth comes continual challenges. The growth trajectory of any entity, be it a business, a ministry, or a relationship, is punctuated with crises. But herein lies the divine design - growth is seldom a linear journey but rather a sequence of troughs and peaks.

The Apostle Paul writes in his letter to the Corinthians, **"There hath no temptation taken you but such as is common to man: but God is faithful, who will not suffer you to be tempted above that ye are able; but will with the temptation also make a way to escape, that ye may be able to bear it." (1 Corinthians 10:13, KJV).** This assures us that every crisis we face is within our capacity to overcome, with **God** ensuring an escape route. However, escape doesn't imply avoidance. Often, the divine escape is through facing the crisis head-on, seeking understanding, growth, and maturation in the process.

Gender dynamics provides another interesting lens to understand the approach to crises. Often, women seek to address every intricacy of a problem, hoping for a comprehensive resolution. This meticulous approach is reminiscent of how **God**, in **His** omnipotence, ensures that every crisis, every challenge, molds us, detail by detail, into **His** intended design.

In the grand tapestry of life, crises are not aberrations, but essential threads woven by the Divine to create a resilient and beautiful fabric of growth and maturity. Instead of shying away from them, it's incumbent upon us, as **God's Mighty Men** and women, to embrace these ordained moments, seeking growth through divine intervention. When faced with challenges, let us take solace in **God's** word, pray for guidance, and steadfastly journey through, knowing that each crisis propels us closer to our divine destiny.

Understanding the Distinctiveness of Men and Women

Throughout history, the unique dynamics between men and women have fascinated philosophers, theologians, and everyday individuals. The Bible, too, provides insights into this distinctiveness, particularly with the creation story where **God** made man and woman, bestowing them with unique qualities and roles. **"So God created man in his own image, in the image of God created he him; male and female created he them." (Genesis 1:27, KJV).** This verse highlights that, while both men and women are created in the image of **God**, they bear distinct attributes that make them different from each other.

One significant difference often observed is in the style of communication. While men tend to be more direct, often providing just the headlines, women, on the other hand, are more detailed-oriented, delving into the fine print. This isn't to stereotype or generalize but is a common observation that plays out in many relationships. Such differences can lead to misunderstandings or even conflicts if not recognized and managed.

Consider a common domestic scenario: a husband returning home after a long day at work. **His** wife, eager to connect, asks about his day. While he might succinctly respond with a 'worked' or a brief headline about a significant event, she might be looking for a more detailed account, craving the intricate details and emotions of his experiences.

This dynamic extends beyond mere verbal communication. When presented with a situation, a man might focus on the overarching elements, much like observing a baby and noting the primary features. A woman, meanwhile, would likely dive deeper, noting and admiring finer details, from the texture of the baby's skin to the curve of its little fingers.

However, it's essential to note that while these differences exist, they aren't a basis for contention but rather a divine design for complementarity. It's about understanding and appreciating these unique attributes. As it says in **1 Peter 3:7 (KJV): "Likewise, ye husbands, dwell with them according to knowledge, giving honour unto the wife, as unto the weaker vessel, and as being heirs together of the grace of life; that your prayers be not hindered."**

Moreover, the distinction between men and women isn't limited to communication alone. It extends to various facets of life, including intimacy. Men are often perceived to be more visually stimulated, while women might be more receptive to touch and sound. Understanding these differences is crucial for a harmonious relationship.

In embracing **God's** design, it's pivotal to acknowledge and appreciate the unique qualities and differences between men and women. Rather than letting these differences be sources of contention, couples can harness them to strengthen their bond, fostering deeper understanding and mutual respect. The Bible reminds us time and again of the value of unity, love, and understanding. By recognizing the divine design in our distinctions and celebrating them, we move closer to fulfilling **God's** purpose for our relationships and lives.

Gentleness: The Measure of God's Mighty Men

In today's world, where aggression and force often dictate the course of human interactions, the concept of gentleness stands as a beacon of **God's** call to love, especially in the realm of marital relationships. The dynamics of a marital bond are profound and require a profound understanding of what it truly means to love. The scriptures emphasize the sanctity of marriage, as stated in **Ephesians 5:25: "Husbands, love your wives, even as Christ also loved the church, and gave himself for it" (KJV).**

The essence of manhood, according to **God's** Word, isn't bound by the stereotypes of physical strength and dominance alone. Instead, the scripture delves deeper into the heart of what makes a man truly **Mighty** in **God's** eyes. This might is observed not in sheer force, but in the gentle touch, the kind word, and the patient spirit.

God's Word clearly articulates the value of gentleness. **"But the fruit of the Spirit is love, joy, peace, longsuffering, gentleness, goodness, faith," as stated in Galatians 5:22 (KJV).** Among these virtues, gentleness stands out as a definitive characteristic of a **God**ly man. As expressed by the Psalmist in **Psalm 18:35: "Thy gentleness hath made me great" (KJV).** The mightiness of a man, in this perspective, isn't determined by the volume of his voice but by the depth of his gentleness.

Moreover, a dichotomy exists within the Christian life. On one hand, Christians are called to be ruthless in their pursuit of righteousness, as evidenced by **Christ**'s statement in **Matthew 5:29-30, "And if thy right eye offend thee, pluck it out, and cast it from thee... And if thy right hand offend thee, cut it off, and cast it from thee" (KJV).** This is a metaphorical call for believers to be fervent and unwavering in eliminating sin from their lives. On the other hand, the same fervor should be transformed into gentleness when dealing with others, especially one's spouse.

In a marital bond, it becomes critical for men to understand the difference between love and lust. While the former cherishes, respects, and nurtures, the latter objectifies and consumes. A wife's need for touch isn't always a call for physical intimacy; sometimes, it's a plea for emotional security and the affirmation of her husband's love. The tenderness with which a husband treats his wife often becomes the bedrock of trust in their relationship.

The modern world, with its distorted perception of masculinity, often overlooks the transformative power of gentleness. But **God's Mighty Men** are those who can wield the sword of righteousness against sin and, simultaneously, cradle their loved ones with the gentle hands of love and care.

The true mightiness in **God's** eyes is gauged by a man's ability to balance his internal ruthlessness against sin with external gentleness towards others. Especially within the sacred confines of marriage, the measure of a man isn't merely in his ability to lead but in his capacity to do so with gentleness. As society continues to redefine masculinity, it is essential for Christian men to root their understanding in the Word of **God** and to aspire to be the kind of **Mighty Men** who exemplify **Christ**'s love through their gentleness.

Living by Faith in a Crystallized World

The scripture is crystal clear in its advocacy for faith as the primary avenue for a relationship with **God**. **Hebrews 11:1** states, **"Now faith is the substance of things hoped for, the evidence of things not seen."** This elucidates that faith isn't merely a belief, but a conviction so profound that it becomes the reality we operate within. But the journey of faith isn't always linear. It demands an evolution, a transition, and sometimes even the audacity to leave behind the old for the new.

It begins with a formalization, a union of those of shared conviction. As it's written in **2 Peter 1:1, "Simon Peter, a servant and an apostle of Jesus Christ, to them that have obtained like precious faith with us through the righteousness of God and our Saviour Jesus Christ."** Associating with those of precious faith is pivotal as it nurtures our growth, letting old relationships transform to foster spiritual maturity.

However, danger lurks in the shadows of this journey. The peril of institutionalizing faith threatens to rob it of its vitality and authenticity. The Bible warns against mere religiosity devoid of genuine faith. In **2 Timothy 3:5,** it mentions, **"Having a form of Godliness, but denying the power thereof: from such turn away."** Falling into routines without grasping the essence of revelation or inspiration is what leads faith communities to institutionalization.

But institutionalization isn't the sole enemy. With age, new barriers arise. It's poignant to remember the human tendencies that steer us away from genuine faith. Youth might be blinded by passion, middle age by pride, and old age by prejudice. Regrettably, the church isn't immune. There are those whose convictions have turned rigid, crystallized in prejudice, leaving them resistant to the fresh winds of revelation.

Yet, **God** in **His** mercy always finds a way to guide **His** flock back to the path of righteousness. The Bible says in **Isaiah 43:19, "Behold, I will do a new thing; now it shall spring forth; shall ye not know it? I will even make a way in the wilderness, and rivers in the desert."** The need for renewal, to rejuvenate our faith, is imperative lest we risk living by works rather than faith.

The emphasis on living by faith cannot be understated. **Romans 1:17** proclaims, **"For therein is the righteousness of God revealed from faith to faith: as it is written, The just shall live by faith."** The Reformation, led by Martin Luther, had its cornerstone in this very principle. Similarly, sanctification, espoused by John Wesley, reshaped faith for many, demonstrating how pivotal revelations can lead to significant spiritual movements.

In the ever-evolving journey of faith, the believer must vigilantly guard against complacency, institutionalization, and prejudice. Embracing faith as the sole foundation ensures a lively, evolving relationship with **God**, continually refreshed by new revelations. As **God's Mighty Men**, the call is clear: to live by faith, ever-seeking **God's** face, and to walk in the light of **His** truth.

"The Power of Identification: God's Mighty Men in Faith"

Throughout history, the evolution of the Church has been marked by shifting paradigms and evolving understandings of **God** and our relationship with **Him.** At every stage, new terminologies, doctrines, and movements emerged to better encapsulate the essence of our rclationship with thc Almighty.

At the turn of the century, we saw the emergence of the word 'power'. This was marked by the outpouring of the Spirit, reminding us of the scriptures in the book of Acts, which proclaim: **"But ye shall receive power, after that the Holy Ghost is come upon you..." (Acts 1:8 KJV).** This era gave rise to a new denomination known as the Pentecostals.

Following this, 'renewal' became the buzzword, leading to the formation of the charismatic movement. The emphasis here was the refreshing and reviving of spiritual gifts and experiences.

Next, we saw a shift from renewal to 'relationship'. This birthed discipleship-focused congregations, a prime example being the church led by Cho in Seoul, Korea. Discipleship, the intentional teaching and following of **Christ**'s ways, became a global phenomenon.

However, every movement has its challenges. As the scriptures warn: **"For there must be also heresies among you, that they which are approved may be made manifest among you." (1 Corinthians 11:19 KJV).** Truth, when taken to its extreme, can become error. Be it enthusiasm, discipleship, or power –

overzealousness in any can lead us astray.

A more recent paradigm shift has been from 'relationship' to 'identification'. This transition birthed the Word Faith movement. A common misconception is that this movement is solely built upon confession. In truth, our identity in **Christ** is established through three cornerstones: Word, Blood, and Spirit. **"And there are three that bear witness in earth, the Spirit, and the water, and the blood: and these three agree in one." (1 John 5:8 KJV).**

In many congregations, the emphasis is predominantly on the redeeming Blood and the indwelling Spirit. However, the Word, which signifies our confession and acknowledgment of **God's** truth, is often neglected. Our identification with **God** is reaffirmed and strengthened through our confession.

For **God's Mighty Men**, their strength lies in the positive. Negative confessions have no place in the heart of a believer. When one says, "I hope I'm saved," or "I hope I'm cleansed by the blood", it lacks conviction. The scriptures affirm: **"That if thou shalt confess with thy mouth the Lord Jesus, and shalt believe in thine heart that God hath raised him from the dead, thou shalt be saved." (Romans 10:9 KJV).**

In contrast, a positive confession such as, "I know I'm saved by the blood", and "I'm living in the kingdom of **God**", reaffirms our position in **Christ**. Such assertions, rooted in the scriptures, are powerful and life-affirming.

The journey of **God's Mighty Men** has always been marked by evolving understandings, terminologies, and movements. While these shifts are instrumental in deepening our relationship with **God**, it is crucial to ensure that we are rooted in the scriptures to avoid falling into error. As we move forward, let our identification be rooted in the Word, redeemed by the Blood, and empowered by the Spirit. And through our positive confessions, may we continually affirm our unshakeable position in the Kingdom of **God**.

Navigating Spiritual Battles with Purpose and Grace

The biblical narrative, laden with timeless wisdom and profound insights, offers a compelling look into the struggles of manhood. The challenges faced by the Israelites on their journey from Egypt to the Promised Land aptly capture the essence of the hurdles we, as men, face in our spiritual journey today.

1 Corinthians 10:1-12 (KJV) reads:

"Moreover, brethren, I would not that ye should be ignorant, how that all our fathers were under the cloud, and all passed through the sea; And were all baptized unto Moses in the cloud and in the sea; And did all eat the same spiritual meat; And did all drink the same spiritual drink: for they drank of that spiritual Rock that followed them: and that Rock was Christ. But with many of them God was not well pleased: for they were overthrown in the wilderness.

Now these things were our examples, to the intent we should not lust after evil things, as they also lusted. Neither be ye idolaters, as were some of them; as it is written, The people sat down to eat and drink, and rose up to play.

Neither let us commit fornication, as some of them committed, and fell in one day three and twenty thousand. Neither let us tempt Christ, as some of them also tempted, and were destroyed of serpents. Neither murmur ye, as some of them also murmured, and were destroyed of the destroyer. Now all these things happened unto them for ensamples: and they are written for our admonition, upon whom the ends of the world are come. Wherefore let him that thinketh he standeth take heed lest he fall."

The aforementioned scripture pinpoints five sins that stymied the Israelites from fully embracing the blessings of Canaan, which are emblematic of the barriers modern men face in reaching their divine potential.

These transgressions are:

Lusting after evil things: The craving for materialistic desires can lead us astray, drawing us away from our spiritual purpose.

Idolatry: Worshipping material objects or placing anything above **God** compromises our faith and derails our spiritual journey.

Fornication: Moral decay weakens our relationship with

God and can fracture the sanctity of our personal relationships.

Tempting Christ: Testing **God's** patience and grace is a perilous act. The Israelites were punished with serpents; we too may face consequences.

Murmuring: Complaining against **God's** will or questioning **His** plans showcases a lack of faith, leading to spiritual pitfalls.

The dichotomy of two spiritual kingdoms – **God's** kingdom of positivity and Satan's realm of negativity – further underscores the importance of making wise choices. By identifying and understanding these roadblocks, we can navigate our spiritual path with purpose and grace, fostering relationships, marriages, and personal growth that resonate with **God's** divine plan.

Embracing manhood through the lens of spirituality is about recognizing and avoiding pitfalls that hinder our spiritual growth. Through the trials and tribulations of the Israelites, we gain a valuable roadmap that, if heeded, can guide us toward maximizing our spiritual potential. As men, the call is clear: align with **God's** positive kingdom, shun the temptations of Satan's negative realm, and embark on a journey of faith, love, and grace. The choices we make, the values we uphold, and the battles we choose to fight determine the men we become – **God's Mighty Men**.

The Kingdom of God and Obedient Spirits: A Reflection on God's Mighty Men

"In the beginning, God created the heaven and the earth." - Genesis 1:1 KJV

From the outset of creation, the divine pattern of **God's** order was laid down. **His** kingdom is one built on principles that are always affirmative, positive, and meant for the edification of **His** creation. **God's** intention when **He** placed Adam in the garden of Eden was to institute **His** principles in man. As the scripture says:

"And the LORD God formed man of the dust of the ground, and breathed into his nostrils the breath of life; and man became a living soul." - Genesis 2:7 KJV

Yet, with the disobedience of Adam, sin entered the world. It is vital to recognize that sin, at its core, is not merely the actions we typically associate with it, such as theft or dishonesty. Rather, sin is fundamentally the denial of **God's** rightful ownership over our lives. It is a spirit of rebellion against the sovereignty of the Almighty.

"For all have sinned, and come short of the glory of God." - Romans 3:23 KJV

Many misinterpret sin as a mere act, such as drinking, adultery, or lying. But the truth of the gospel message is profound: the true nature of sin is unbelief in the **Lord Jesus Christ**. It is not merely the actions that condemn, but the heart of unbelief from which such actions emanate.

"But without faith it is impossible to please him: for he that cometh to God must believe that he is, and that he is a rewarder of them that diligently seek him." - Hebrews 11:6 KJV

Central to the Kingdom of **God** is peace – a peace that surpasses human understanding. This peace is foundational and only spirits aligned with obedience can maintain it. The Bible speaks to this peace, stating:

"And the peace of God, which passeth all understanding, shall keep your hearts and minds through Christ Jesus." - Philippians 4:7 KJV

Thus, **God's** Kingdom will never permit a spirit of disobedience. As with a household where one disobedient child can disrupt the harmony, in the vast expanse of heaven, even one rebellious spirit can break the peace.

The importance of obedience and repentance cannot be overstated. The Kingdom of **God** welcomes only those who have acknowledged their sins, repented, and put their faith in the **Lord Jesus Christ**. For as the scripture says:

"That if thou shalt confess with thy mouth the Lord Jesus, and shalt believe in thine heart that God hath raised him from the dead, thou shalt be saved." - Romans 10:9 KJV

God's Mighty Men are those who understand the weight of obedience, the power of faith, and the importance of aligning their spirits with **God's** purpose. Only through belief in **Jesus Christ** and submission to **His** will can we hope to attain the peace that heaven promises. It is not mere actions, but the very spirit of obedience and faith that ensures our place in the Kingdom of **God**. As we reflect on our lives, let us strive to be obedient spirits, upholding the peace and principles of **God's** Kingdom.

The Principles of the Kingdom: A Reflection on God's Mighty Men

"For as by one man's disobedience many were made sinners, so by the obedience of one shall many be made righteous." - Romans 5:19 KJV

The biblical narrative is rich with stories of mankind's relationship with the Divine, providing tales of trial, redemption, and the ongoing battle between good and evil. This teaching examines the juxtaposition of **God's** Kingdom versus the kingdom of Satan, emphasizing the powerful principles at the foundation of these kingdoms.

1. Adam's Fall and Its Implications

From the very beginning, Adam's transgression against **God** bore significant consequences. Not merely was he cast out of the Edenic paradise, but the spiritual implications of this action are profound.

"And the Lord God said, Behold, the man is become as one of us, to know good and evil: and now, lest he put forth his hand, and take also of the tree of life, and eat, and live for ever: Therefore the Lord God sent him forth from the garden of Eden, to till the ground from whence he was taken." - Genesis 3:22-23 KJV

With Adam's ejection from Eden, mankind was essentially expelled from the Kingdom of **God**. The dominion and deep communion initially granted to man was forfeited, and Satan capitalized on this lapse, assuming control.

2. Jesus, the Second Adam

It was not until the arrival of **Jesus**, often referred to as the second Adam, that this dominion was wrested back from Satan's grasp.

"And having spoiled principalities and powers, he made a show of them openly, triumphing over them in it." - Colossians 2:15 KJV

Through **Jesus**, those who believe and accept Him have their relationship with the Kingdom of **God** restored. In **Him,** the principles of the Kingdom, symbolizing the very keys to heaven, are illuminated and provided to mankind.

3. Kingdom Principles

Throughout scripture, it is evident that **God's** word offers a blueprint for living a righteous life. **"All scripture is given by inspiration of God, and is profitable for doctrine, for reproof, for correction, for instruction in righteousness." - 2 Timothy 3:16 KJV**

When one reflects on these principles, it becomes evident that they serve as cornerstones for a harmonious and just society. Attributes such as honesty, loyalty, and truthfulness are foundational tenets of the Kingdom of **God**. Without these principles, society lacks the spiritual tools to thrive and flourish.

4. The Perversion of Principles in a Fallen World

Adam's fall resulted in a perversion of these principles, leading to a world steeped in negativity and corruption. Mankind, without **God's** guidance, is fundamentally negative in nature.

"Behold, I was shapen in iniquity; and in sin did my mother conceive me." - Psalm 51:5 KJV

However, even in this fallen state, remnants of these principles can be discerned, whether in secular philosophies or societal norms. These vestiges of the Kingdom's principles are a testament to their universal appeal and intrinsic value.

God's Mighty Men, as exemplified through figures like Adam and **Jesus**, provides a roadmap for understanding humanity's relationship with divinity. The principles of the Kingdom of **God** stand as beacons of hope, guiding individuals toward righteousness. While the world may be tainted by Adam's original sin, **Jesus**'s sacrifice offers a path of redemption, enabling believers to access and embody the principles of the Kingdom once more.

"Being confident of this very thing, that he which hath begun a good work in you will perform it until the day of Jesus Christ." - Philippians 1:6 KJV

The Power of Agreement and Manhood

In the divine realm, the ability to reconcile, unite, and reach a mutual consensus holds the essence of empowerment. The biblical ethos underlines the importance of agreement and reconciliation, portraying it as a path to spiritual power. This teaching will dissect the power of agreement and the concepts of manhood with references to the scriptures.

The fundamental principle of any ministry is the emphasis on unity and harmony. One might find these concepts familiar, as they lie at the heart of Christianity, preceding the new revelations that we continually receive. A prevailing notion suggests that in life, "it's not what you know but who." This statement poses a critical query: How does one achieve salvation and enter the Kingdom of Heaven?

"Jesus saith unto him, I am the way, the truth, and the life: no man cometh unto the Father, but by me."

(John 14:6, KJV). Hence, the journey to heaven isn't solely grounded on knowledge but rather on recognizing **Jesus Christ**. This realization reiterates the correctness of the earlier principle when it remains unperverted.

The spiritual realm operates on the lordship of **Jesus Christ**, while in the secular domain, individuals tend to become their own lord, leading to the distortion of spiritual principles. When **God** created humanity, the guiding principle was to seek pleasure in pleasing **God**. But with mankind's perversion, the focus shifted to self-gratification, birthing habits driven by personal pleasure.

Among **God's** many creations, **He** devised the act of sex as a pleasurable experience. **"Marriage is honourable in all, and the bed undefiled:" (Hebrews 13:4, KJV). God's** intention was clear: to make the act enjoyable, leading to procreation and thus ensuring the continuity of the human race. The underlying principle is that true joy emerges from challenges or sorrows. In the Gospel according to John, this philosophy is outlined: **"A woman when she is in travail hath sorrow, because her hour is come: but as soon as she is delivered of the child, she remembereth no more the anguish, for joy that a man is born into the world." (John 16:21, KJV).**

Reiterating the concept: All true joy is born out of sorrow. The journey of life is filled with challenges and sorrows, from the rigors of education to the complexities of relationships. Yet, enduring these challenges leads to profound joy and accomplishments.

Marriage, for instance, mirrors this principle. The act of committing oneself to another is rife with challenges, yet the resulting union brings immeasurable joy. Choosing a life partner comes second only to the paramount decision of accepting **Christ** as one's savior. Thus, making wise choices, founded on the teachings of **Christ**, paves the way for a fulfilled life.

In the grand narrative of spirituality and manhood, the power of agreement and the principles of manhood stand out. Recognizing **Jesus Christ** as the savior, prioritizing Him over personal desires, and understanding life's pleasures and challenges are all instrumental in leading a spiritually enriched life. By aligning our choices with the teachings of the scriptures, we not only find true joy but also embrace **God's** purpose for us.

A Study of Marriage Through the Lens of Scripture

Marriage, as understood in its divine essence, bears witness to the profound spiritual journey's individuals undertake on this earth. Many liken it to experiences that mirror the vast contrasts of heaven and hell, pointing to the profound joy and sometimes agonizing challenges that this sacred bond can encapsulate.

It has been observed by many that marriage is, indeed, the closest reflection of heaven or hell on this terrestrial realm.

"And he answered and said unto them, Have ye not

read, that he which made them at the beginning made them male and female, And said, For this cause shall a man leave father and mother, and shall cleave to his wife: and they twain shall be one flesh?" (Matthew 19:4-5 KJV)

In the course of ministering, countless testimonies bear witness to this sentiment. There are accounts of men who have braved the fiery trials of marriage, while others have tasted the blissful delights of a harmonious union. For the young man standing at the crossroads of his future, the imperative lesson is this: If you desire a virtuous wife, let your supplications begin now.

The act of praying is not merely to be treated as a casual afterthought post-marriage. It is, instead, an ongoing commitment, an earnest act of seeking divine intervention in anticipation of the life partner **God** has set apart.

"Delight thyself also in the Lord; and he shall give thee the desires of thine heart." (Psalm 37:4 KJV)

The lack of specificity in prayer is a pitfall many unwittingly walk into. Vague requests usher in ambiguity. **God**, in **His** infinite wisdom, responds to the heart's deepest desires with precision. Therefore, let clarity and discernment define your prayers.

Moreover, it is a perilous assumption for women to believe that a man's intrinsic nature would undergo transformation post-marriage. In echoing the sentiments found in Scripture, one is reminded that it isn't a wife's duty to change her husband.

"What therefore God hath joined together, let not man put asunder." (Matthew 19:6 KJV)

A prevailing misconception is that a wife can draw a man to **God**, molding him in her image. This displacement from **God's** design for mankind to be in **His** image gives rise to strains in marital relationships.

"And God said, Let us make man in our image, after our likeness: and let them have dominion... So God created man in his own image, in the image of God created he him; male and female created he them." (Genesis 1:26-27 KJV)

It is beyond the domain of any wife to convict her husband of sin. Such conviction is reserved for the Holy Ghost. Interferences by spouses in this divine process can yield resentment, leading to fissures in communication and relational harmony.

"And when he is come, he will reprove the world of sin, and of righteousness, and of judgment." (John 16:8 KJV)

The pursuit of a righteous relationship, grounded in mutual respect, understanding, and divine principles, is a reflection of **God's** design for marriage. Praying with specificity, understanding the sanctity of the marital bond, and acknowledging the divine order can pave the way for marital unions that truly reflect heaven on earth. Above all, let the Spirit lead, for in **His** guidance, both men and women can find the path to a marriage that mirrors the love, grace, and unity **God** intended.

A Study in Spiritual Transformation

As people embark on the journey of spiritual growth, there's often an emphasis on personal change – a transition from old habits to new, from worldly desires to spiritual ambitions, and from self-centered living to **God**-centered life. One of the most profound experiences in this journey is understanding the true power of transformation that comes from **God**.

"For by grace are ye saved through faith; and that not of yourselves: it is the gift of God:" - Ephesians 2:8 (KJV)

This line is a powerful reflection of our human tendencies. We often judge others by their actions, yet ourselves by our intentions. This creates a dissonance in our relationships, leading to disagreements over seemingly trivial matters, such as household chores or responsibilities. It's easy to point fingers and lay blame, but the heart of the matter often lies deeper. Our habits may be subject to change, but our inherent nature – our soul, our essence – is a domain where only the Divine can truly work wonders.

"Create in me a clean heart, O God; and renew a right spirit within me." - Psalms 51:10 (KJV)

Transformation is a necessity. In the realm of spiritual

understanding, the Kingdom of **God** operates on principles that stand in stark contrast to the world we live in. Our world is a place of perversion and distortion. To align ourselves with the Kingdom of **God**, we must undergo a conversion – not just in belief, but in every aspect of our lives, from our thoughts and emotions to our very appearances.

God has set forth a challenge, especially to the men, urging them to be the pillars of change. They are called to lead by example, forging a path of spiritual growth not just for themselves but for their families and communities.

"But be ye doers of the word, and not hearers only, deceiving your own selves." - James 1:22 (KJV)

In, the path to spiritual growth and transformation is one of self-awareness, acceptance, and an unwavering trust in **God's** ability to change our nature. While the world might focus on superficial alterations, true change arises from a divine intervention. **God's Mighty Men** are those who recognize this divine truth, embrace it, and live by it, inspiring others along the way.

"I can do all things through Christ which strengtheneth me." - Philippians 4:13 (KJV).

CHAPTER SEVEN

God's Mighty Men: The Power of Positive Faith

The transformative power of positive faith cannot be overstated. At the core of our very being, we are wired to respond, understand, and resonate more deeply with affirmations than negations. In our everyday lives, from the realm of business to the more profound spiritual journey, the interplay between negativity and positivity is evident.

Take for instance the salesman. How many times has a salesman walked into a room, only to be met with initial resistance and skepticism? Most people's first instinct is to doubt, to challenge, to resist. But for a deal to be closed, that initial resistance must be turned into acceptance—a conversion from the negative to the positive. In the Bible, a clear representation of this conversion can be seen. As stated in **Proverbs 18:21 (KJV), "Death and life are in the power of the tongue: and they that love it shall eat the fruit thereof."** This scripture underlines the profound power that our words and affirmations hold.

Jesus, in **His** infinite wisdom and boundless love, came into our lives as the ultimate converter. **He** sought to transform our natural negative inclinations into positive affirmations of faith and belief. In **Matthew 7:24-27 (KJV), Jesus** illustrates the importance of building our lives on a solid foundation:

"Therefore whosoever heareth these sayings of mine, and doeth them, I will liken him unto a wise man, which built his house upon a rock: And the rain descended, and the floods came, and the winds blew, and beat upon that house; and it fell not: for it was founded upon a rock. And every one that heareth these sayings of mine, and doeth them not, shall be likened unto a foolish man, which built his house upon the sand: And the rain descended, and the floods came, and the winds blew, and beat upon that house; and it fell: and great was the fall of it."

Building one's life on negativity is akin to building on sand—unstable and fleeting. But rooting oneself in the unwavering positivity of **God's** love and word is like building on solid rock.

God's presence is magnified in positivity. **He** dwells in our praises, as echoed in **Psalm 22:3 (KJV): "But thou art holy, O thou that inhabitest the praises of Israel."** For **God** to bless and inhabit our marriages, relationships, and endeavors, our approach and attitude must be one of positivity and praise.

However, acknowledging the negative without actively working to convert it into a positive leaves a void. **Jesus** warns in **Matthew 12:43-45 (KJV)** that when an unclean spirit is cast out and returns to find its former home empty, it brings along even more spirits:

"When the unclean spirit is gone out of a man, he walketh through dry places, seeking rest, and findeth none. Then he saith, I will return into my house from whence I came out; and when he is come, he findeth it empty, swept, and garnished. Then goeth he, and taketh with himself seven other spirits more wicked than himself, and they enter in and dwell there: and the last state of that man is worse than the first."

This powerful lesson underscores the need to not only cast out the negative but actively replace it with the positive. Whenever we confess our sins and shortcomings, it becomes essential to immediately affirm our faith and righteousness through scripture.

The journey of faith is an ongoing conversion from negativity to positivity. By recognizing the power of positive faith and continuously seeking to align our lives with **God's** teachings, we invite **His** blessings, protection, and guidance. Our words, beliefs, and actions hold immense power, and as **God's Mighty Men** and women, we must endeavor to harness this power for good, for growth, and for glorifying the Almighty.

A Study on Leadership and God's Mighty Men

"All the characteristics of a kingdom emanate from the character of the king." This profound statement captures the essence of leadership, as understood through biblical principles. Within the sacred texts of the Holy Bible, one can discern the paramount importance of character and leadership.

"Righteousness exalteth a nation: but sin is a reproach to any people." - Proverbs 14:34 KJV

The character of the king, the paramount leader, determines the ethos, culture, and demeanor of the kingdom. A kingdom that is led by righteousness will reflect that goodness in all its dealings. Conversely, a leadership that is rooted in wickedness will result in a kingdom steeped in malfeasance.

The scriptures affirm the significant influence of a leader on their followers. In the context of a church, a pastor, embodying the king or leader, has a palpable effect on the congregation. The home, too, is not exempt from this principle. The character of the head of the family significantly shapes the overall dynamic and environment of the home.

"Train up a child in the way he should go: and when he is old, he will not depart from it." - Proverbs 22:6 KJV

Leadership, especially in a familial setting, bears the weighty responsibility of training and guiding younger generations. When the leader of the home lacks **God**ly character and resorts to punishing children for flaws reflective of their own, it perpetuates a cycle of negative behavior. These shortcomings become evident in the children, who often replicate the character traits and behaviors they witness.

The Bible underscores the necessity for leaders to exemplify **Christ**-like character:

"Let this mind be in you, which was also in Christ Jesus." - Philippians 2:5 KJV

However, when recognition within a family is solely linked to negative behavior, it creates an environment where negative actions become a means to gain attention. In the wider societal context, this can result in destructive behaviors and actions.

This insight reminds us of the significance of **God**ly leadership and the dire consequences of a lack thereof. It emphasizes the critical importance for men, especially those in positions of influence, to cultivate a character rooted in **Godliness** and Christlikeness.

Leadership, as revealed through the scriptures, is not merely about authority but about the character of the one leading. As **Christ** serves as the ultimate example of righteous leadership, so too must men aim to reflect **His** likeness in their roles as leaders. By understanding and embodying the character of **Christ**, leaders can create environments that thrive in love, understanding, and righteousness. It is this character that will raise up generations that honor **God**, promote peace, and foster love among all.

"And he shall be like a tree planted by the rivers of

water, that bringeth forth his fruit in his season; his leaf also shall not wither; and whatsoever he doeth shall prosper." - Psalms 1:3 KJV.

The Role of the Father in Fostering Faith

"Train up a child in the way he should go: and when he is old, he will not depart from it." (Proverbs 22:6 KJV)

The scripture emphasizes the significance of early teachings and guidance, stressing that they leave lasting imprints on a child's heart and mind. Thus, every father who raises children must be acutely aware of the immense responsibility he shoulders.

Balance is the linchpin of a fulfilling life. Equally vital is the ability of every father to strike a balance between admonishing the wrong and celebrating the right. It's a biblical tenet that the rod and reproof give wisdom, but a child left to himself bringeth his mother to shame **(Proverbs 29:15 KJV).** However, constant chastisement without acknowledgment of their achievements can foster resentment and rebellion.

"For whom the Lord loveth he chasteneth, and scourgeth every son whom he receiveth." (Hebrews 12:6 KJV)

This verse underscores the importance of loving

correction, but correction alone is not enough. A father's affirmative words are powerful, molding his children's perception of themselves. If they constantly hear only rebukes, children may develop a skewed sense of worth, where they might believe that wrongdoing is the sole avenue to garner their father's attention.

Many fathers aspire for their offspring to walk in **God's** righteous path. Their earnest cries echo David's prayer, **"Give me understanding, and I shall keep thy law; yea, I shall observe it with my whole heart." (Psalm 119:34 KJV).** But aspirations alone are futile if actions don't corroborate. Faith, without works, is dead. Many fathers tend to compartmentalize their religious duties to the confines of the church walls, creating a dichotomy between church life and home life. This disparity sends mixed messages to their young ones.

Reading scriptures, worshiping, and praying are fundamental tenets of the Christian faith. Yet, they must permeate the household. A father mustn't just be a beacon of faith in church but an embodiment of **Christ**'s teachings at home. James rightly said, **"But be ye doers of the word, and not hearers only, deceiving your own selves." (James 1:22 KJV)**. A father's piety mustn't be restricted to Sunday sermons; it must manifest in daily life, in actions, in words, and in lessons taught at the dinner table.

When fathers delegate their divine duties, relegating them to pastors, teachers, or other professionals, they abdicate their spiritual leadership in the home. Instead of fostering faith, this can inadvertently breed a culture of hypocrisy, as children discern a chasm between professed beliefs and lived realities.

Being a father is a divine calling, a role ordained by **God** to shepherd, guide, nurture, and lead the family. Just as **God** the Father loves, disciplines, guides, and remains ever-present for **His** children, earthly fathers are called to reflect that divine love and guidance in their homes. As fathers strive to imbue their homes with **God**ly virtues, they lay a foundation for their children, ensuring they not only walk in faith but remain steadfast in it, becoming **God's Mighty Men** and women of the future.

A Call to Authentic Manhood

Throughout history, **God's** design has been for leaders, particularly spiritual leaders, to guide, disciple, and nurture those under their care. In the traditional Christian context, the pastor's role is pivotal in the spiritual growth of his congregation. Scripturally, Paul writes in **Ephesians 4:11-12 (KJV): "And he gave some, apostles; and some, prophets; and some, evangelists; and some, pastors and teachers; For the perfecting of the saints, for the work of the ministry, for the edifying of the body of Christ."** This underscores the importance of these leaders in guiding and molding believers.

However, in today's world, there seems to be an over-reliance on these church leaders, particularly the pastor, to take on the spiritual responsibility of entire families. This is a deviation from **God's** ideal pattern. Families, especially men, are to play an active role in spiritually nurturing their homes. The unfortunate reality is that many delegate this responsibility, hoping that an hour in church might undo the spiritual negligence exhibited throughout the week. Yet, **Proverbs 22:6 (KJV)** reminds us, **"Train up a child in the way he should go: and when he is old, he will not depart from it."**

The aspiration to be **God**ly men is universal among believers. This longing, though earnest, often remains an unfulfilled desire because of the unwillingness to confront one's shortcomings and take proactive steps towards spiritual growth. To truly change, it is crucial to face reality and hear from **God** directly. **Romans 10:17 (KJV)** says, **"So then faith cometh by hearing, and hearing by the word of God."** A testament to the power of **God's** word is evident in the transformative experience of Tom Dooley's brother, who, upon hearing the divine word, gave his heart to **Christ**.

Prophets hold a special place in this transformative journey. Their role, often confrontational and challenging, is to shake believers out of their comfort zones, urging them to align with **God's** will. The scriptures contain numerous accounts of prophets who paved the way for deliverance. **Judges 6:8 (KJV)** reads, **"That the Lord sent a prophet unto the children of Israel, which said unto them, Thus saith the Lord God of Israel, I brought you up from Egypt, and brought you forth out of the house of bondage."** Here, a prophet was sent before Gideon's emergence as a deliverer. Similarly, before **Jesus**' ministry, John the Baptist prepared the way, as mentioned in **Matthew 3:3 (KJV): "For this is he that was spoken of by the prophet Esaias, saying, The voice of one crying in the wilderness, Prepare ye the way of the Lord, make his paths straight."**

However, the words of prophets, as sharp and piercing as they might be, should be weighed and balanced. Pastors often serve this purpose, providing a temperate perspective to prophetic revelations. **1 Thessalonians 5:20-21 (KJV)** advises, **"Despise not prophesyings. Prove all things; hold fast that which is good."**

In this era, where the cry for gender equality and inclusivity is at its peak, there's a need to refocus on the unique spiritual roles and responsibilities of men. Men, as leaders of their households, must embody Christlikeness, drawing their families closer to **God**.

The call to authentic manhood is a call to spiritual leadership, accountability, and growth. While pastors, prophets, and church leaders play critical roles in our spiritual journey, the onus of spiritual nurturing at home rests squarely on the shoulders of men. Embracing this divine mandate will not only transform individual lives but also leave a lasting spiritual legacy for generations to come.

Call to Courage and Leadership in an Age of Indecision

In today's world, men often face challenges that threaten their roles, identities, and confidence. The call for strong, decisive, and **God**ly leadership is imperative. It's not about diminishing the importance or roles of women, but rather about men rising to the roles **God** has designed for them. The essence of a man, according to biblical teachings, is marked by courage, wisdom, and the favor of **God**.

God's Favor and Wisdom
Every man needs **God's** favor in his life. Favor isn't merely about receiving blessings, but it is a divine enablement to carry out **God's** plans. This favor is found in **God's** promise: **"And all these blessings shall come on thee, and overtake thee, if thou shalt hearken unto the voice of the LORD thy God" (Deuteronomy 28:2 KJV).**

Moreover, wisdom is essential. Proverbs, known as the book of wisdom, provides insights into the life of a man. **"For length of days, and long life, and peace, shall they add to thee" (Proverbs 3:2 KJV)**. It promises that wisdom brings **"riches, and honour" (Proverbs 8:18 KJV),** as well as pleasure and peace.

The Imperative of Courage
Courage is the third and pivotal element in a man's life. Why? Here are five reasons:

#1 Facing Reality: It's not always easy to face the truths of our existence. It might be pain, past failures, or any range of challenges. However, "Be strong and of a good courage; be not afraid, neither be thou dismayed: for the LORD thy **God** is with thee whithersoever thou goest" (Joshua 1:9 KJV).

#2 Admitting Needs: Contrary to societal expectations, real strength is found in vulnerability and acknowledging our needs.

#3 Making Decisions: Decisiveness is an attractive trait and an important one too. Making informed decisions requires courage.

Leadership in Relationships: This involves understanding the desires of your partner and acting on them decisively. It's not about dominance but about cherishing, understanding, and making choices that benefit the

In an era where indecision, passivity, and compromise seem to be the norm, **God's** call for **His** men to stand strong, be decisive, and lead with courage is ever more urgent. The journey of a man is not to diminish the role of women but to stand beside them, leading with **God's** favor, wisdom, and courage. The scriptures remind us of our divine heritage and potential, and it's high time men answered this call, showcasing the strength and decisiveness that is needed in our world today.

Stewards of Change in the Kingdom

"What? know ye not that your body is the temple of the Holy Ghost which is in you, which ye have of God, and ye are not your own?" - 1 Corinthians 6:19 (KJV)

The divine mandate for man, as expressed in scriptures and passed down through generations, has remained constant. **God's** purpose for man has always been clear, and **He** has placed a heavy responsibility upon them to lead and be stewards in all spheres of life. This teaching delves into this divine calling and the importance of understanding and walking in it for today's man.

In the Holy Bible, there are three distinct roles that **God** has ordained for men: to guide, guard, and govern. This triad of responsibilities is foundational for understanding man's purpose in family, church, business, and community.

"Husbands, love your wives, even as Christ also loved the church, and gave himself for it;" - Ephesians 5:25 (KJV)

1. To Guide: A guide is one who shows the way by leading or advising. The man's role is to provide direction, clarity, and spiritual leadership. This is not just for his family, but also in every space he occupies. By leading with wisdom and understanding, he ensures that those he's responsible for walk in the light of **God**.

2. To Guard: The role of a guard is to protect against

harm or danger. It's crucial for men to stand as shields for their families, defending them from physical, emotional, and spiritual threats. This guarding also extends to the words spoken within and about the family. As stewards of **God's** word, men should uplift and value their wives and children, understanding that their words have the power to build or break.

"Death and life are in the power of the tongue: and they that love it shall eat the fruit thereof." - Proverbs 18:21 (KJV)

3. To Govern: To govern means to control, influence, or regulate. This doesn't imply dictatorship but rather wise stewardship. It's a call for men to take charge, be decisive, and ensure there's order and progress.

However, to effectively guide, guard, and govern, one must introspect and initiate personal change. Many times, the chaos and negativity in our environments reflect our internal turmoil. It's essential to understand that change begins from within.

"And why beholdest thou the mote that is in thy brother's eye, but considerest not the beam that is in thine own eye?" - Matthew 7:3 (KJV)

For many, personal transformation is a journey fraught with trials, temptations, and tests. Still, through perseverance and a sincere desire to align with **God's** will, change is attainable. Many have walked this path, fallen, risen, and come out refined.

God's Mighty Men are not just figures of the past but are present in today's age, continually wrestling with their imperfections and seeking alignment with the divine mandate. Through introspection and reliance on **God's** grace, these men understand that true change can ripple out from them, positively affecting their families, businesses, and communities. By embracing the roles **God** has ordained for them, men can indeed be **Mighty** stewards in the kingdom, fostering love, protection, and growth wherever they are placed.

"I can do all things through Christ which strengtheneth me." - Philippians 4:13 (KJV)

The Kingdoms of Light and Darkness: A Discourse on God's Mighty Men

The essence of spiritual warfare, as told in the scriptures, is the conflict between two kingdoms. One is the Kingdom of Light, and the other, the Kingdom of Darkness. But before understanding these realms, one must first comprehend the nature of the King who rules the Kingdom of Light – **God**. The Bible tells us that, **"This then is the message which we have heard of him, and declare unto you, that God is light, and in him is no darkness at all." (1 John 1:5 KJV)**

The Kingdom of Light

The fundamental characteristics of **God's** Kingdom are profoundly positive because they mirror the nature of **God** Himself:

Light: In **God's** Kingdom, light prevails. **"God is light."** This is not just physical luminance, but spiritual and moral brightness. The Apostle John confirms this in thc scriptures: **"And the light shineth in darkness; and the darkness comprehended it not." (John 1:5 KJV)**

Holiness: God is the epitome of holiness. It's said, **"But as he which hath called you is holy, so be ye holy in all manner of conversation; Because it is written, Be ye holy; for I am holy." (1 Peter 1:15-16 KJV)**

Truth: The truth is an intrinsic part of **God's** character. **Jesus Christ** himself affirmed, **"I am the way, the truth, and the life." (John 14:6 KJV)**

Love: One of the most celebrated verses of the Bible professes **God's** love: **"For God so loved the world, that he gave his only begotten Son, that whosoever believeth in him should not perish, but have everlasting life." (John 3:16 KJV)**

Life: God is the source of all life. **"In him was life; and the life was the light of men." (John 1:4 KJV)**

Faith and Obedience: Faith in **God** leads to obedience, as the Apostle Paul wrote, **"For in Jesus Christ neither circumcision availeth any thing, nor uncircumcision; but faith which worketh by love." (Galatians 5:6 KJV)**

The Kingdom of Darkness

Contrastingly, the Kingdom of Darkness is characterized by:

Darkness: Instead of light.
Sin: As opposed to holiness.
Lies: In place of truth.
Hatred or Malice: Instead of love.
Death: Opposite of life.
Disobedience: As opposed to obedience.

Human nature leans towards disobedience, as evidenced by the need for parents to teach their children obedience. This is testament to Paul's observation in Romans, **"For all have sinned, and come short of the glory of God;" (Romans 3:23 KJV)**

The parable of the prodigal son from **Luke 15:11-32 KJV** is a profound depiction of the journey from rebellion against the Kingdom of Light towards ruin, and then the pathway to reconciliation with the Father. This pattern is cyclic: Rebellion, Ruin, Repentance, Reconciliation, and Restoration.

Understanding the stark contrasts between the Kingdom of Light and the Kingdom of Darkness illuminates the journey of **God's Mighty Men**. These men are not just soldiers on a battlefield but are souls in the spiritual warfare of life, constantly navigating between these two kingdoms. As believers, the goal is to embrace the positive attributes of **God's** Kingdom, drawing nearer to

His light, truth, and love, while resisting the pull of darkness, lies, and death. Only then can one truly be a part of **God's Mighty** battalion, striving towards eternal reconciliation and restoration.

The Power of Repentance and Redemption

The trajectory of mankind is deeply punctuated with themes like rebellion, ruin, repentance, reconciliation, and restoration. This cyclical pattern can be witnessed in the annals of human history, reflected in personal narratives, and, most importantly, delineated within the sacred scriptures.

The pivotal point between ruin and reconciliation is undoubtedly repentance. It stands as the doorway to mending, a bridge from destruction to restoration. Without repentance, reconciliation remains out of reach.

"If we confess our sins, he is faithful and just to forgive us our sins, and to cleanse us from all unrighteousness." (1 John 1:9 KJV). Repentance is the turning point that determines whether one remains in ruin or advances towards reconciliation with **God**.

As mentioned, one cannot overlook the gravity of repentance in the Christian faith. This is evident in the very onset of **Jesus**'s ministry. **He**, being the embodiment of a prophet, priest, and king, heralded the message of repentance. **"From that time Jesus began to preach, and to say, Repent: for the kingdom of heaven is at**

hand." (Matthew 4:17 KJV). Jesus's declaration underscores the inescapable truth that repentance is not just important—it is paramount.

However, a person doesn't merely enter the kingdom of **God** through merit. It's not a matter of being "good enough." Instead, it's about acknowledging the shortfall, recognizing the missed mark of **God's** glory, and then taking deliberate action to change course.

"For all have sinned, and come short of the glory of God;" (Romans 3:23 KJV).

The sacrifice of **Jesus** at Calvary serves as the monumental testament to **God's** judgment and mercy. **God's** judgment declared mankind deserving of eternal separation due to sin. Yet, in an act of unparalleled love, **He** also judged mankind worthy of salvation, granting **Jesus Christ** to bear the sins of humanity.

"For God so loved the world, that he gave his only begotten Son, that whosoever believeth in him should not perish, but have everlasting life." (John 3:16 KJV).

It is vital to understand that **God's** judgment was pronounced at Calvary, and now, individuals stand before the commandment to repent. A failure to obey this command showcases a spirit of rebellion. As a result, one effectively judges themselves, deciding their eternal destination based on their response to **Christ**'s redemptive work.

Pastors, evangelists, and teachers who truly grasp the weight of this truth often find themselves overwhelmed. It's not a matter of business success or failure; it's the very essence of eternity, life, and death. It's the eternal dichotomy of heaven and hell.

God's Mighty Men understand the profundity of repentance and its quintessential role in bridging ruin and reconciliation. The biblical blueprint, culminating in the work of **Jesus** at Calvary, reveals the intertwining themes of judgment and grace. As believers, the responsibility lies in recognizing the gravity of the gospel, responding in repentance, and reaching out to a world in desperate need of restoration. The challenge is clear, and the stakes are eternal. For in the ebb and flow of rebellion and restoration, repentance stands firm as the beacon of hope.

The Pillars of His Kingdom

The gravity of the spiritual journey is not one to be taken lightly. Just as children engage in the play of marbles with frivolity, the game of life and the pursuit of **God's** kingdom is serious, demanding our full commitment and unwavering dedication. For in this journey, the stakes are high, and the rewards even higher. **God's** call is not merely for our happiness, success, or fellowship, though these are cherished byproducts. At the core of the gospel is an invitation to forge an intimate relationship with **Jesus Christ**.

"But seek ye first the kingdom of God, and his righteousness; and all these things shall be added unto you." - Matthew 6:33 (KJV)

Repentance serves as the bedrock of spiritual growth. It allows us to purge the negative, the sin, and the worldly distractions, making way for divine positivity. If we aspire for our families and societies to flourish in a **God**ly manner, this divine positivity becomes indispensable. Only through embodying **Christ**-like character can **God's Mighty** work manifest in our societies, fortifying our families and communities.

"If we confess our sins, he is faithful and just to forgive us our sins, and to cleanse us from all unrighteousness." - 1 John 1:9 (KJV)

This kingdom, **God's** kingdom, operates on principles that are profound yet simple: the keys to the kingdom. And at the helm of this divine kingdom is none other than the **Lord**, beckoning us to transition from a life centered around self to one that seeks to please **Him.** When we redirect our intentions to please **God**, we align with **His** will, which always champions our highest good. Nothing **God** does is arbitrary; every move is orchestrated for our utmost benefit.

"And we know that all things work together for good to them that love God, to them who are the called according to his purpose." - Romans 8:28 (KJV)

Our human perspective is often limited, and we may

grapple to understand the broader purpose behind the trials we face. Yet, **God**, in **His** infinite wisdom, employs every circumstance, be it favorable or adverse, molding it for our ultimate benefit. By entrusting our lives and challenges to **Him,** we enable **His** transcendent glory to work miracles, transforming adversities into blessings, as evident in the life of Joseph.

"But as for you, ye thought evil against me; but God meant it unto good, to bring to pass, as it is this day, to save much people alive." - Genesis 50:20 (KJV)

The journey to aligning with **God's Mighty** purpose demands more than passive faith. It calls for intentional repentance, relentless commitment, and an unwavering trust in **His** divine plan. When we pivot from a self-centered existence to one that seeks to please the **Lord**, we not only experience the byproducts of happiness, success, and fellowship but also tap into **God's** transformative power, which consistently aims for our highest good. As **God's Mighty Men**, we become the bedrock upon which **His** kingdom flourishes, showcasing **His** transcendent glory.

The Balance of Humility and Blessing

The concept of divine balance is evident in scriptures, where **God's Mighty Men** have time and time again showcased the intrinsic value of humility. The intertwining of humility and blessing formulates the basis upon which **God's** kingdom operates. It defines a relationship with **God** that transcends materialistic gain and dives deep into spiritual enrichment.

"And we know that all things work together for good to them that love God, to them who are the called according to his purpose." - Romans 8:28 (KJV)

This scripture illustrates that **God's** perspective on "good" transcends our earthly understanding. Many perceive "good" in the materialistic sense, such as the comforts of life symbolized by Cadillacs and spacious homes. While it's undoubtedly more comfortable to ride in a Cadillac and live in a four-bedroom home, the essence of **God's** blessings is not limited to material prosperity.

"Not that I speak in respect of want: for I have learned, in whatsoever state I am, therewith to be content. I know both how to be abased, and I know how to abound: everywhere and in all things, I am instructed both to be full and to be hungry, both to abound and to suffer need." - Philippians 4:11-12 (KJV)

The Apostle Paul's experience, as articulated in Philippians, mirrors this sentiment. **He** acknowledges the comforts of abundance while also recognizing the profound lessons derived from seasons of lack. Life's different vehicles, whether they be grand cars or smaller ones, are merely temporary vessels. What remains essential is the humility we carry with us on our journey.

"Humble yourselves in the sight of the Lord, and he

shall lift you up." - James 4:10 (KJV)

There's an undeniable spiritual principle reflected in the scriptures: the act of humbling oneself before **God**. This humble stance is not a mere act of submissiveness, but a powerful position of alignment with **God's** will. The principle that humility precedes blessing is a recurring theme throughout the Bible, reminding us that to be exalted by **God**, one must first be grounded in humility.

But why is humility so crucial in **God's** eyes? When one exalts oneself, they place their trust, hope, and pride in their capabilities, thereby sidelining **God**. But when one humbles themselves, they acknowledge the need for **God**, inviting **His** guidance and blessings into their life. Humbling oneself is, in essence, a posture of receptivity.

In, while the world may measure success and blessings through tangible assets and comforts, **God's** scale of blessing is founded on the spiritual growth and character of a person. The life of **God's Mighty Men** is a testament to this balance, showing that in humility, lies the path to divine blessing. True exaltation comes not from elevating oneself but from lowering oneself in humble submission to **God's** will, allowing Him to do the lifting.

Humility Precedes Blessing

"Humble yourselves in the sight of the Lord, and he

shall lift you up." - James 4:10 KJV

Throughout the annals of history, both secular and scriptural, there is a recurring theme that shows the power of humility. Those who humble themselves before **God**, acknowledging their weaknesses and need for divine guidance, are often the ones who receive profound blessings and achieve great things in the name of the **Lord**. A prime illustration of this can be found in the story of a Christian broadcaster.

I recall a poignant moment when a well-known Christian broadcaster, facing accusations from the SEC, was emotionally shattered. The allegations were that he had been dishonest regarding an investment piece. These allegations were far from the truth. The broadcaster was an embodiment of truthfulness and integrity, and these accusations deeply pained him.

The media was quick to sensationalize the event, and headlines splashed with words such as "...... accused of fraud." Imagine the heartbreak of a man known for his honesty and integrity. The scene of him sitting at his home, head in hands, tears streaming down, is not one of defeat, but one of profound humility.

But the story does not end there. From that valley of despair emerged a vision and drive that catapulted his into a global network. The scripture beautifully says, **"For his anger endureth but a moment; in his favour is life: weeping may endure for a night, but joy cometh in the morning." - Psalm 30:5 KJV**. Indeed, for this broadcaster, the morning brought forth joy and a vision to expand.

Such stories echo the wisdom of the Bible, which time and again stresses the importance of humility. The Bible says, **"Pride goeth before destruction, and a haughty spirit before a fall." - Proverbs 16:18 KJV.** The opposite is also true. Humility often goes before elevation.

Why does **God** value humility so? It is because, in our humility, we acknowledge that it is not by our might, but by **His**. We recognize that all the blessings we receive, the visions we have, and the works we accomplish are not ours but **His**. **God** warns us, saying, **"I am the LORD: that is my name: and my glory will I not give to another, neither my praise to graven images." - Isaiah 42:8 KJV.**

For those of us, the question posed resonates deeply. How many feel a sense of humility, a gentle nudging from **God** that something significant is on the horizon? This world is fraught with temptations and tribulations, from greed to lust to wars and diseases. But as believers, if we anchor ourselves in humility and trust in **God's** plan, we are destined to receive **His** blessings.

Humility is more than a virtue; it is a conduit for **God's** blessings. As illustrated by the story of Pat Robertson, even in moments of profound pain and humility, **God's** plan is always for our elevation. For all who are humble in spirit and trust in the **Lord**, blessings await. As believers, let's keep our hearts open to **God's** teachings, remain steadfast in our faith, and remember always that humility precedes blessing.

"When pride cometh, then cometh shame: but with the lowly is wisdom." - Proverbs 11:2 KJV

The Worthiness of Jesus and the Transformation He Offers

In the intricate tapestry of the world, there lies a portion dominated by negativity, evil works, and malevolence. Such is the sphere where most of humanity finds solace, lost in its dark corridors and away from the divine embrace. **"Wherein in time past ye walked according to the course of this world, according to the prince of the power of the air, the spirit that now worketh in the children of disobedience" (Ephesians 2:2, KJV).**

However, with the advent of **Jesus**, the second Adam, a transformational shift was offered to mankind. **He** bore our sins upon the cross, offering salvation to those who sought refuge from the chains of wickedness. The message was profound: **"Come unto me, all ye that labour and are heavy laden, and I will give you rest" (Matthew 11:28, KJV). His** sacrifice offered an opportunity for a changed mindset, a renewed heart, and a translation into **God's** kingdom.

With this new allegiance, an individual no longer merely belongs to the world but becomes an heir to **God's** magnificent kingdom. **"And if children, then heirs; heirs of God, and joint-heirs with Christ; if so be that we suffer with him, that we may be also glorified together" (Romans 8:17, KJV).** The joys of this inheritance are beyond worldly treasures. But alas, self-doubt often permeates, making one feel unworthy or incapable.

However, worthiness in the eyes of **God** is not determined by one's deeds or merits but rather through the righteousness of **Jesus Christ. "But of him are ye in Christ Jesus, who of God is made unto us wisdom, and righteousness, and sanctification, and redemption" (1 Corinthians 1:30, KJV).** Our worth is intertwined with **Jesus**, making us deserving of heavenly blessings not through our righteousness, but **His**.

When believers truly internalize this truth, the revelation is transformative. It liberates from feelings of unworthiness, emphasizing that our worth is embedded in **Jesus Christ**. **"I am crucified with Christ: nevertheless I live; yet not I, but Christ liveth in me: and the life which I now live in the flesh I live by the faith of the Son of God, who loved me, and gave himself for me" (Galatians 2:20, KJV).**

Reflecting on personal journeys, it's clear how **Jesus** offers a way out of the quagmire of negativity. From a life marred in hopelessness, the touch of **Jesus** can elevate one to a state of grace, love, and positivity.

The worthiness of **Jesus** is our beacon in a world laden with challenges. It is through Him that believers find their true worth and the strength to overcome adversities. Regardless of past afflictions or negative tendencies, in **Jesus**, there's an avenue for change, renewal, and unwavering hope. It is essential, then, to recognize and embrace the transformation **He** offers, making us not just men but **God's Mighty Men**, empowered and equipped for every good work. **"For we are his workmanship, created in Christ Jesus unto good works, which God hath before ordained that we should walk in them" (Ephesians 2:10, KJV)**.

CHAPTER EIGHT
The Power of Faith and Truth

Throughout the course of history and in our personal journey of faith, a constant concept we grapple with is the undeniable power of faith. Faith is the unwavering belief in what is unseen. It transcends our human understanding and connects us to the divine. How often do we question the validity of what we cannot tangibly perceive? They never, for it's what we call faith. It's that indomitable spirit which allows us to declare, "When the word of God becomes more real to me than my circumstance." This is the point where the spoken promises and edicts of the Almighty become more substantial than the evident challenges around us.

One profound passage in the of the Bible reflects this sentiment: **"Now faith is the substance of things hoped for, the evidence of things not seen" (Hebrews 11:1 KJV).**

Our experiences often form the bedrock of our faith. Personal testimonies, such as the realization of healing through the stripes of Jesus, serve as a testament to the transformative power of faith. It is written, **"But he was wounded for our transgressions, he was bruised for our iniquities: the chastisement of our peace was upon**

him; and with his stripes we are healed" (Isaiah 53:5 KJV). Every believer will face moments of doubt, instances where they have to fight for their healing, for their promises, because as it is written, **"The thief cometh not, but for to steal, and to kill, and to destroy" (John 10:10a KJV).**

This battle is not of flesh and blood, but it is spiritual. The enemy thrives in deception. Pondering the ancient scriptures, one might wonder about the great rebellion in heaven, where Lucifer, the once radiant angel, led astray a third of the angelic host. Such cunning, such deception. How was it possible?

This spiritual conflict and the battle against deception is highlighted in **John 8:44 (KJV): "Ye are of your father the devil, and the lusts of your father ye will do. He was a murderer from the beginning, and abode not in the truth, because there is no truth in him. When he speaketh a lie, he speaketh of his own: for he is a liar, and the father of it."**

The Word of God is the truth, and it is through this Word that believers are set free. The scriptures state, **"So then faith cometh by hearing, and hearing by the word of God" (Romans 10:17 KJV).** The Word has transformative power, for **"For the word of God is quick, and powerful, and sharper than any twoedged sword, piercing even to the dividing asunder of soul and spirit, and of the joints and marrow, and is a discerner of the thoughts and intents of the heart" (Hebrews 4:12 KJV).**

A personal journey with Christ showcases the power of the truth in the Word. When the Word of God is consumed, internalized, and lived out, it acts as the liberator from the chains that once held us captive. The addictive habits, the past mistakes, and the overwhelming challenges – they lose their grip.

Life's journey is fraught with challenges, temptations, and battles. However, with faith as our shield and the truth of God's word as our sword, we can overcome. The journey of faith isn't a path void of struggles. Still, it's a path where every challenge faced is met with the unwavering belief that God's word is truer than our current reality. It is the journey of a believer who holds onto the truth, who immerses themselves in the Word of God, and finds true freedom. As we walk this path, may our faith ever increase, and may the truth of God's word ever guide our steps.

A Testament of Transformation through Christ

"But as many as received him, to them gave he power to become the sons of God, even to them that believe on his name:" - John 1:12 (KJV)

The transformative power of **Jesus Christ** in a believer's life is profound. It is a journey from darkness to light, from despair to hope, and from sin to righteousness. It is the process of being born again, of having a renewed mind and heart, and of being translated into the kingdom of **God**.

"But the natural man receiveth not the things of the Spirit of God: for they are foolishness unto him: neither can he know them, because they are spiritually discerned." - 1 Corinthians 2:14 (KJV)

As a testament to this transformation, I declare: Jesus came into my life and renewed my mind. Through this spiritual regeneration, my heart has been transformed. I have been translated into the kingdom of **God**. I confess that I have been born again and, at this very moment, I am identified with **Jesus Christ**. This identity is affirmed by **His** word, **His** precious blood, and by the Spirit.

"The Spirit itself beareth witness with our spirit, that we are the children of God: And if children, then heirs; heirs of God, and joint-heirs with Christ; if so be that we suffer with him, that we may be also glorified together." - Romans 8:16-17 (KJV)

In the present, I am an heir of **God** and a joint heir with **Jesus Christ**. The indwelling **Christ** assures me that every need in my life is met through the worthiness of **Jesus**.

"For ye are bought with a price: therefore glorify God in your body, and in your spirit, which are God's." - 1 Corinthians 6:20 (KJV)

Christ lives in me and I in **Him.** Because of this union, I am assured that every need is met by my Father through the worthiness of **Jesus. His** worthiness is undeniable. In **Him,** I find my worth.

Yet, in areas of my life where there are negatives and characteristics that need alteration, I need to repent. With humility, I need to turn from them and confess them out of my life. Sin and negativity have no place in a heart surrendered to **Christ**.

"And if we confess our sins, he is faithful and just to forgive us our sins, and to cleanse us from all unrighteousness." - 1 John 1:9 (KJV)

In the name of **Jesus**, I receive a fresh anointing of the Holy Ghost. With gratitude, I acknowledge that as a child of **God**, the faith of **Jesus Christ** resides in my heart. The overwhelming love of **God**, made manifest through **Jesus Christ**, fills my heart. I am grateful for the continuous work **He** is doing in my life.

The journey with **Christ** is one of daily renewal, repentance, and reliance on **His** sufficiency. It's a testament to the transformative power of **Jesus Christ** in the life of believers. To be identified with **Him,** to share in **His** inheritance, and to be infused with **His** love and faith are privileges that come with surrendering to **His** lordship. And in this posture of surrender and gratitude, we can unashamedly and without any embarrassment, praise Him for **His** goodness and mercy in our lives.

Patterns, Principles, and Power in the Kingdom

"What? know ye not that your body is the temple of the Holy Ghost which is in you, which ye have of God, and ye are not your own?" - 1 Corinthians 6:19 (KJV)

As we delve into 1 Corinthians 10, it is crucial to identify the five sins that act as barriers, preventing us from achieving our full potential in spiritual manhood. Regardless of our physical location, the spiritual barriers we face are universal.

In an early chapter, it was established that two moral or spiritual kingdoms exist: the kingdom of **God** and the kingdom of Satan. The character of each kingdom emanates from its core essence.

"The earth is the LORD's, and the fullness thereof; the world, and they that dwell therein." - Psalms 24:1 (KJV)

Everything in **God's** kingdom is positive and righteous, reflecting **His** pure and holy nature. In contrast, Satan's kingdom is rife with negativity and darkness. But remember, **God** always builds on a positive note, never on a negative. If any negativity exists in our lives, when committed to **God**, by **His** magnificent glory, **He** transforms it for our good.

"And we know that all things work together for good to them that love God, to them who are the called according to his purpose." - Romans 8:28 (KJV)

God never dwells in negativity; **He** inhabits the positive. Praises uplift **Him,** and as it's written, **"But thou art holy, O thou that inhabitest the praises of Israel." - Psalms 22:3 (KJV).** Flattery, a pseudo form of praise, is always negative as it harbors concealed hostility.

The book of Proverbs provides insights into the virtues men ought to embody. Primarily, favor stands out as the chief among them, followed by other essential attributes. There are principles that every man needs to grasp:

#1. Communication is the basis of life.
#2. Exchange represents process.
#3. Balance is key.
#4. Agreement holds power.

"Can two walk together, except they be agreed?" - Amos 3:3 (KJV)

Disagreement weakens and saps power. In contrast, agreement fortifies and instills power. It's a divine truth that agreement breeds power, just as knowledge translates into authority, and decisions transform into energy.

"The fear of the LORD is the beginning of knowledge: but fools despise wisdom and instruction." - Proverbs 1:7 (KJV)

In our journey as **God's Mighty Men**, it is paramount to understand the patterns and principles **God** has laid out. Everything **He** orchestrates, **He** does according to a divine pattern. Recognizing and aligning with these patterns ensures that we walk in harmony with **His** will and purpose.

In becoming **God's Mighty Men**, understanding the duality of spiritual kingdoms and embracing divine patterns and principles is paramount. Armed with knowledge, decision-making prowess, and the power of agreement, we can harness the energy and authority required to overcome barriers and ascend to our full spiritual manhood potential. Let us walk in the light of **God's** word, and may **His** favor be upon us as we navigate the journey of life in alignment with **His** kingdom's principles. Amen.

"Thy word is a lamp unto my feet, and a light unto my path." - Psalms 119:105 (KJV).

The Kingdom Principle of Commitment

Everything **God** does, **He** does according to a principle. Each action of **God** is governed by a guiding truth. All the positive principles of human society upon which it stands firmly are derived from kingdom principles. The kingdom of Satan lacks these grounding tenets. **"Wherein in time past ye walked according to the course of this world, according to the prince of the power of the air, the spirit that now worketh in the**

children of disobedience" (Ephesians 2:2 KJV).

Thus, if we, as followers of **Christ**, intend to live a life aligned with these principles, we must delve deep into the Scriptures. For, **"All scripture is given by inspiration of God, and is profitable for doctrine, for reproof, for correction, for instruction in righteousness" (2 Timothy 3:16 KJV).**

Through faith and action based on these principles, we open the doors of heaven. It's the unwavering faith in **Christ** and the belief that because **He** is worthy of all, we too become inheritors of **His** grace and worthiness. This symbiotic relationship with **Christ** identifies us in three profound ways: Word, Love, and Spirit. **"For there are three that bear record in heaven, the Father, the Word, and the Holy Ghost: and these three are one" (1 John 5:7 KJV).**

The keystone of this discourse is the principle that "You're committed to what you confess." This isn't just a mere statement; it's a truth resonated throughout the Bible. Commitment, as illustrated by matrimonial vows, is sacred. Declining to take these vows often signifies a reluctance to make lasting commitments. **"Therefore shall a man leave his father and his mother, and shall cleave unto his wife: and they shall be one flesh" (Genesis 2:24 KJV).**

Affirmations of love and commitment in a marital relationship are pivotal. The Bible teaches us, **"Husbands, love your wives, even as Christ also loved the church, and gave himself for it" (Ephesians 5:25**

KJV). For a woman, emotional security is intricately tied to her feeling of uniqueness, knowing she is singular in her husband's eyes. This is why the institution of marriage was created monogamously, emphasizing the importance of fidelity and exclusivity.

In, commitment, in both our spiritual walk and earthly relationships, is crucial. Through **God's** teachings and the principles, **He** laid down, we understand the sanctity of promises made, the weight of words uttered, and the depth of love professed. To be **God's Mighty Men** and women, we must embrace these principles and manifest them in our lives, serving as beacons of **His** eternal love and wisdom.

The Kingdom Principle of Commitment

Everything **God** does, **He** does according to a principle. Each action of **God** is governed by a guiding truth. All the positive principles of human society upon which it stands firmly are derived from kingdom principles. The kingdom of Satan lacks these grounding tenets. **"Wherein in time past ye walked according to the course of this world, according to the prince of the power of the air, the spirit that now worketh in the children of disobedience" (Ephesians 2:2 KJV).**

Thus, if we, as followers of **Christ**, intend to live a life aligned with these principles, we must delve deep into the Scriptures. For, **"All scripture is given by inspiration of God, and is profitable for doctrine, for**

reproof, for correction, for instruction in righteousness" (2 Timothy 3:16 KJV).

Through faith and action based on these principles, we open the doors of heaven. It's the unwavering faith in **Christ** and the belief that because **He** is worthy of all, we too become inheritors of **His** grace and worthiness. This symbiotic relationship with **Christ** identifies us in three profound ways: Word, Love, and Spirit. **"For there are three that bear record in heaven, the Father, the Word, and the Holy Ghost: and these three are one" (1 John 5:7 KJV).**

The Journey from Egypt to Canaan

In the divine intricacy of **God's** creation, the relationship between man and woman was laid out with utmost precision. We are told in the scripture, **"But I would have you know, that the head of every man is Christ; and the head of the woman is the man; and the head of Christ is God" (1 Corinthians 11:3, KJV).** This very scripture highlights the sacred hierarchy and the interdependent roles that men and women play in the divine scheme of things.

The woman was created, not as a competitor but as a complement to man. **"And the LORD God said, It is not good that the man should be alone; I will make him a help meet for him" (Genesis 2:18, KJV).** However, a significant component of this relationship is reciprocity. While a woman's submission to a man is a divine design, it is equally pivotal for the man to cherish, nurture, and minister to her needs.

Failure to fulfill these roles often leads to disruption in marital harmony. It's not uncommon for individuals to seek external sources of validation and fulfillment when their primary relationship is lacking. This manifests in various ways – from a wife's inclination towards soap operas as an escape, to a man seeking solace outside the marital fold.

Yet, genuine love, as spoken about in the scriptures, isn't merely a passionate affair. **"Greater love hath no man than this, that a man lay down his life for his friends" (John 15:13, KJV). Jesus** emphasized obedience and sacrifice over fleeting emotions. The worldly understanding of love often equates it with lust or temporary infatuation. But divine love – the agape love – is a selfless, sacrificial, and unconditional love.

Drawing parallels with 1 Corinthians 10, our journey in understanding manhood can be likened to the Israelites' exodus from Egypt to Canaan. This migration wasn't just physical but symbolic of a spiritual awakening, of breaking free from the chains of the past, and marching towards the Promised Land. Just as the Israelites faced trials, temptations, and tests on their journey, men today face numerous challenges in understanding and fulfilling their divine roles.

Being aware of one's flaws and seeking transformation is the mark of **God's Mighty Men**. It's the act of recognizing the negatives and striving for righteousness.

As said in **James 4:8, KJV, "Draw nigh to God, and he will draw nigh to you. Cleanse your hands, ye sinners; and purify your hearts, ye double minded."**

The divine design of relationships and roles is clear in the scriptures. Man, as the leader, is entrusted with the responsibility to not only lead but also to cherish, nurture, and minister to the needs of the woman. The road to true manhood is paved with challenges, temptations, and tests, but with faith in **God** and an understanding of **His** Word, it is a journey that leads to blessings and fulfillment. Just as **God** led the Israelites to the Promised Land, **He** guides **His Mighty Men** today, directing them towards righteousness, love, and divine purpose.

The Topology and Power of Spiritual Deliverance

"Study to shew thyself approved unto God, a workman that needeth not to be ashamed, rightly dividing the word of truth." - 2 Timothy 2:15 (KJV)

In the sacred Scriptures, we uncover spiritual truths woven with remarkable depth, providing profound revelations for those who earnestly seek. As exhorted in **2 Timothy 2:2**, our calling as believers extends beyond our personal journey with **Christ**; we are to disciple and educate others, ensuring the propagation of faith across generations. This study delves into the typology found in

1 Corinthians 10, with its roots firmly anchored in the Old Testament.

The Old Testament presents Egypt as a powerful representation of the world, a world where the children of Israel found themselves in oppressive bondage. This bondage symbolizes the weight and chains of sin.

"For all have sinned, and come short of the glory of God;" - Romans 3:23 (KJV)

Under the authoritarian rule of Pharaoh, their lives were marred with hardships. Pharaoh, in this spiritual analogy, stands as a type of Satan. The children of Israel, representing humanity, were trapped in the world, ensnared by sin, and under Satan's dominion.

But in this bleak landscape shines the hope of deliverance. The final plague, the death of the firstborn, was a looming terror. However, **God** provided a way out for **His** chosen people. Through the application of lamb's blood on the doorposts, a divine shield was created.

"And the blood shall be to you for a token upon the houses where ye are: and when I see the blood, I will pass over you, and the plague shall not be upon you to destroy you, when I smite the land of Egypt." - Exodus 12:13 (KJV)

This Passover symbolism directs our attention to **Jesus Christ**, the ultimate lamb of **God**. **His** blood wasn't spilled in vain but served as the key to everlasting life.

"The thief cometh not, but for to steal, and to kill, and to destroy: I am come that they might have life, and that they might have it more abundantly." - John 10:10 (KJV)

The common misconception that one must first rectify all wrongdoings before approaching **God** is flawed. Redemption begins with a genuine relationship with **God**, who then empowers us to overcome the chains of our sins.

"Come unto me, all ye that labour and are heavy laden, and I will give you rest." - Matthew 11:28 (KJV)

The story of **God's Mighty Men**, as symbolized by the children of Israel, offers a profound understanding of spiritual truths. It reveals the reality of our bondage to sin, the deceptive dominion of Satan, but more importantly, the boundless love and grace of our **Lord**. Just as the Israelites were redeemed from physical bondage, we too can be delivered from spiritual chains through **Christ**'s sacrifice. May we, emboldened by this knowledge, rise as **God's Mighty Men** and women, perpetuating the teachings of **Christ** and bringing light to those ensnared in darkness.

The Power of Transformation through Divine Intervention

"In the LORD put I my trust: how say ye to my soul, Flee as a bird to your mountain?" - Psalm 11:1 (KJV)

It is often misconstrued by many that one must first become morally righteous and sanctified to approach the divine throne of **God**. However, this notion contradicts the very essence of the Almighty's love and mercy. A commonly held belief says one should "get good to get to **God**." However, the truth is vastly different – one must get to **God**, and in **His** mercy, **He** refines and sanctifies us.

"But God commendeth his love toward us, in that, while we were yet sinners, Christ died for us." - Romans 5:8 (KJV)

This transformative journey from being bound in chains of our own doing to experiencing true liberation through **God's** grace is awe-inspiring. This transformation, akin to being lifted from the "gutter" and placed in the "uttermost," is a testament to **God's** transcendent glory.

"Being justified freely by his grace through the redemption that is in Christ Jesus:" - Romans 3:24 (KJV)

There is an illustrative reference to the blood applied while the Israelites were still in Egypt. This blood symbolizes salvation. The Israelites didn't wait to be out of Egypt to have the blood applied. Likewise, salvation reaches us while we are still entrenched in our sins. The very act of salvation transforms a sinner into a saint.

"For by grace are ye saved through faith; and that not of yourselves: it is the gift of God:" - Ephesians 2:8 (KJV)

Yet, within the sacred confines of the church, many are hesitant to admit their flaws, fearing judgment from their peers. But here's the truth: each one of us, at some point, has faltered. Everyone has "blown it." And the understanding that "we've all blown it" is not just an acknowledgment of our human frailties but also a testament to the abundant grace of **God** that covers us all.

"If we confess our sins, he is faithful and just to forgive us our sins, and to cleanse us from all unrighteousness." - 1 John 1:9 (KJV)

The underpinning of sin lies in unbelief. The strength of sin stems from pride, and its character is rooted in deceitfulness. And it is this very pride that acts as a barrier between man and **God**. It prevents us from confessing, repenting, and transforming.

"Pride goeth before destruction, and a haughty spirit before a fall." - Proverbs 16:18 (KJV)

However, when we, as **God's** creation, realize our worth in **His** eyes and acknowledge **His** supreme craftsmanship in our lives, we embrace a transformative power. A power that's not of this world, but of a heavenly realm, promising change, renewal, and redemption.

"Behold, I will do a new thing; now it shall spring forth; shall ye not know it? I will even make a way in

the wilderness, and rivers in the desert." - Isaiah 43:19 (KJV)

The journey of **God's Mighty Men** is not one of self-righteousness but one of divine intervention and transformation. It's a testament to the boundless love and mercy of our Creator who meets us right where we are – in our mess, in our imperfections, in our sins – and then elevates us to become reflections of **His** glory. It's an invitation to shed the weight of pride, embrace the humility of repentance, and experience the life-altering touch of **God's** transcendent glory. And in this spiritual dance, as we surrender, we find ourselves not lost, but found, not diminished, but magnified in **His Mighty** image. Amen.

A Journey from Sin to Sanctification

The tale of humanity is a profound testament to **God's** enduring mercy and transformative power. When the Divine Artist first fashioned man, he saw that it was good. Our blueprint, Adam, was born into imperfection. The scripture reminds us**, "So God created man in his own image, in the image of God created he him; male and female created he them" (Genesis 1:27 KJV).** The symphony of creation reverberated with the perfection of Adam, which is an echo of what humanity once was and could be once again through **Christ**.

Our existence is intrinsically tied to the legacy of Adam. Yet, through **Jesus Christ**, the second Adam, humanity has been offered a second chance to reclaim that original glory. As it is written, **"For as in Adam all die, even so in Christ shall all be made alive" (1 Corinthians 15:22 KJV).** This truth ought to be more than just a distant doctrine; it should stir our souls and impel us to act.

The Bible counsels us to be **"wise as serpents and harmless as doves" (Matthew 10:16 KJV).** Wisdom isn't just knowledge; it's the application of that knowledge. And in the application, we find salvation. The magnitude of salvation is realized in recognizing our sinful nature. For only those who acknowledge their need for **God** can truly experience **His** salvation. As **Romans 5:8 KJV** says, **"But God commendeth his love toward us, in that, while we were yet sinners, Christ died for us."**

The Exodus of the Israelites from Egypt paints a vivid picture of this journey of salvation. Their escape from Pharaoh through the Red Sea symbolizes our liberation from sin. As the Red Sea enveloped the enemies of Israel, so does the waters of baptism bury our old sinful selves. The wilderness period that follows is a testament to sanctification, an essential process in a believer's life. This is akin to the testing and refinement of faith, as illustrated in **Deuteronomy 8:2 KJV**, **"And thou shalt remember all the way which the Lord thy God led thee these forty years in the wilderness, to humble thee, and to prove thee, to know what was in thine heart, whether thou wouldest keep his commandments, or no."**

But **God's** purpose isn't to leave us wandering in the

wilderness. **His** intention is to lead us into the Promised Land. The crossing of the Jordan River represents the outpouring of the Holy Spirit upon believers, and entering Canaan signifies entering **God's** rest, our divine inheritance.

However, the journey from sin to sanctification isn't without its challenges. All works of the flesh revealed in Galatians chapter 5, including an unrenewed mind are roadblocks. **1 Corinthians 6:9-11 KJV** elucidates, **"Know ye not that the unrighteous shall not inherit the kingdom of God? Be not deceived: neither fornicators, nor idolaters, nor adulterers, nor effeminate, nor abusers of themselves with mankind… And such were some of you: but ye are washed, but ye are sanctified, but ye are justified in the name of the Lord Jesus, and by the Spirit of our God."**

The narrative of **God's Mighty Men** isn't just a tale of old. It's the narrative of each of us, navigating through the complexities of life, sin, and redemption. From Adam's fall to **Christ**'s resurrection, from the Israelites' exodus to their entry into Canaan, we are reminded of **God's** overarching plan for humanity: salvation, sanctification, and ultimate union with **Him.** As believers, we are called not to merely spectate but to actively participate, embrace the transformative power of **Christ**, and embark on this spiritual journey towards **God's** Promised Land.

Journey to Canaan Land

In the biblical narrative, Canaan land stands as an emblematic representation of promise, potential, and divine fulfillment. It is a land where **God** envisioned **His** people to prosper, thrive, and actualize the vast promises **He** had for them. **"For all the promises of God in him are yea, and in him Amen, unto the glory of God by us." (2 Corinthians 1:20, KJV).** The Old Testament paints a vivid picture of the Israelites' journey to Canaan, a journey that was filled with trials, tests, and triumphs.

Yet, its full spiritual realization is manifested in the New Testament, specifically in the book of Acts, where believers, through the baptism of the Holy Ghost, enter into a divine rest. This rest denotes a cessation from worldly works and a profound reliance on the promises of **God**. As Hebrews states, **"Let us therefore fear, lest, a promise being left us of entering into his rest, any of you should seem to come short of it." (Hebrews 4:1, KJV).**

At the heart of this spiritual journey lies two powerful forces: faith and fear. Both are invisible, intangible, yet they govern our actions, decisions, and ultimately, our destinies. At first glance, faith and fear might seem to be opposites, but on deeper introspection, they share a fundamental definition. They both revolve around the belief in the unseen. As stated in Hebrews, **"Now faith is the substance of things hoped for, the evidence of things not seen." (Hebrews 11:1, KJV).** Fear, on the other hand, also believes in the unseen but in a negative, debilitating manner. While faith believes in the positive realization of unseen promises, fear dreads the unseen potential threats.

The power of these forces cannot be underestimated. Just as faith has the power to attract blessings, opportunities, and positive outcomes, fear, conversely, has the potency to repel, hinder, and bring about negative consequences. This concept is vividly illustrated in everyday life, from the confidence (or lack thereof) we exude in job interviews to our interactions with animals. It's an age-old principle: what we project is what we often attract. If we approach life with faith and confidence, we are more likely to attract positive outcomes. However, if we let fear dominate our actions, we often find ourselves in unfavorable situations.

The quest for peace is a noble endeavor, and it is one that requires men of goodwill. The Scriptures provide insight into this: **"Glory to God in the highest, and on earth peace, good will toward men." (Luke 2:14, KJV).** The key here is "goodwill." Peace can only reign among men of goodwill, and the transformation into such men comes through a profound relationship with **God**, through **His** son **Jesus Christ**. It's a transformative journey from being self-centered to being **Christ**-centered, from being fearful to being faithful.

The narrative of Canaan land and the principles of faith and fear offer profound spiritual insights into our walk with **God**. Just as the Israelites had to overcome numerous challenges to reach their promised land, we too face our own giants, be they doubt, fear, or external adversities. However, by grounding ourselves in faith, by believing in the promises of **God**, and by nurturing a deep relationship with **Him,** we can reach our own Canaan land – a place of divine fulfillment, peace, and promise. As we journey through life, may we be ever reminded to walk by faith, not by sight, and to rely on the Almighty, who is the source of all blessings and the dispeller of all fears.

Armor of Righteousness and the Adversary's Arsenal

Throughout the annals of history and scripture, there have been tales of **Mighty Men** and women who stood firm in their faith, acting as beacons of light amidst the world's darkest hours. These individuals, guided by a profound spiritual conviction, understood a foundational truth: the power of fear and the relentless adversary that seeks to exploit it.

Our contemporary world bears witness to the influence of fear, whether through global politics or individual decisions. It reminds one of the biblical assertion that **"For God hath not given us the spirit of fear; but of power, and of love, and of a sound mind." (2 Timothy 1:7, KJV)**. Fear, especially when it drives us to act, can attract precisely what we dread most.

Leaders who advocate for peace often confront this conundrum. They yearn for harmony, yet they recognize that showing vulnerability can attract malevolent forces.

In the spiritual realm, this principle holds as well: when we fear the devil, we inadvertently give him an avenue of attack.

Jesus, in **His** profound wisdom, articulated this when **He** declared, **"the prince of this world cometh, and hath nothing in me" (John 14:30, KJV).** This powerful statement indicates that because **Jesus** was without sin, the devil found no foothold in **Him.** Similarly, Satan finds strength where sin resides in our hearts. **His** dominion extends wherever transgressions linger.

The redeeming message of the Gospel, however, is that through **Christ**, we can attain a semblance of **His** sinlessness. By accepting **Him,** confessing our sins, and being washed by **His** blood, we are shielded from the devil's grasp. As stated in **1 John 1:7, "But if we walk in the light, as he is in the light, we have fellowship one with another, and the blood of Jesus Christ his Son cleanseth us from all sin" (KJV).** In this state of sanctified grace, we can rebuke the devil, and he shall flee from us.

Yet, it's essential to recognize the subtle weapons in the devil's arsenal: temptation and accusation. Temptations, fleeting and relentless, can besiege even the most devout. The Bible cautions us that **"But every man is tempted, when he is drawn away of his own lust, and enticed" (James 1:14, KJV)**. Nevertheless, being tempted is not the downfall; succumbing to it is. Even when our minds wander into forbidden territories, invoking **Christ**'s name and righteousness can steer us back onto the path of purity.

However, the devil's second weapon, accusation, is potent, aiming to ensnare our minds with guilt and self-doubt. As believers, it is paramount to remember that through **Christ**'s sacrifice, our slate has been wiped clean. **"There is therefore now no condemnation to them which are in Christ Jesus, who walk not after the flesh, but after the Spirit" (Romans 8:1, KJV)**. Even if fleeting thoughts steer us away momentarily, our salvation remains intact as long as our hearts stay anchored in **Christ**.

The saga of **God's Mighty Men** and women serves as a testament to the enduring battle between righteousness and the forces that seek to undermine it. By embracing **Christ**'s redemptive love, grounding ourselves in the scriptures, and recognizing the adversary's tactics, we can navigate life's trials with unwavering faith and fortitude. Like the **Mighty** heroes of yore, we too can stand tall, cloaked in **God's** armor, and deflect the fiery darts of the wicked.

Battling Temptation and Accusation with the Shield of Faith

The age-old battle between man and spiritual adversity has been the essence of countless narratives in scriptures. The **Mighty Men** of **God**, as portrayed in scriptures, were not just warriors of physical battles, but also valiant soldiers in the spiritual realm. The battle of the mind, in particular, is one of the most complex arenas where these **Mighty Men** defended themselves against the enemy.

"For as he thinketh in his heart, so is he." - Proverbs 23:7 (KJV)

From this scripture, it is evident that the heart is where true intentions and convictions reside. The devil, ever so cunning, uses half-truths to ensnare us, making us feel guilty for mere thoughts. But one must discern the difference between fleeting temptations of the mind and the convictions of the heart. To be tempted is not sin; giving in to temptation is.

"Let no man say when he is tempted, I am tempted of God: for God cannot be tempted with evil, neither tempteth he any man." - James 1:13 (KJV)

Temptations will come, as they did for **Jesus** in the wilderness, but our response to these temptations defines our spiritual strength. The devil, as both tempter and accuser, will attempt to penetrate our defenses. However, **God** has equipped us with the shield of faith.

"Above all, taking the shield of faith, wherewith ye shall be able to quench all the fiery darts of the wicked." - Ephesians 6:16 (KJV)

This verse from Ephesians exemplifies that the shield of faith is our defense mechanism against the devil's tactics. To wield this shield effectively, one must stand firm in the word of **God**, refuting every lie with the truth of scripture. By declaring with conviction, as mentioned, "I am a man of **God**," we affirm our position and reject the devil's lies.

Every believer, whether a new convert or a seasoned Christian, faces challenges in their thought life. The key to overcoming them is to understand their nature. As stated, “I rejected it out of my mind,” showcases the importance of actively repelling un**God**ly thoughts and not allowing them to take root in the heart.

"There is therefore now no condemnation to them which are in Christ Jesus, who walk not after the flesh, but after the Spirit." - Romans 8:1 (KJV)

Every believer has the assurance that in **Christ Jesus**, they are free from condemnation. This freedom is not just from the external bondage of sin but also from the internal chains of guilt and accusation. By proclaiming, "I'm free, **Lord**, in the name of **Jesus**," believers establish their victory in **Christ**.

In, the **Mighty Men** of **God** stand not only as warriors in physical battles but more importantly, as overcomers in the spiritual realm. The battle of the mind is fierce, but with the shield of faith and the word of **God** as our sword, victory is assured. Embrace the truth of the scriptures, understand the tactics of the enemy, and stand firm in the freedom **Christ** provides. For in **Christ**, we are more than conquerors.

"Nay, in all these things we are more than conquerors through him that loved us." - Romans 8:37 (KJV)

Walking in Faith and Victory

In the realm of spiritual warfare, there stands a battle between the forces of good and the forces of darkness. Those who understand their identity in **Christ** are better equipped to face these challenges, resisting the devil's deceptions and standing firm in their faith.

The devil, as an accuser, is relentless in his attempts to undermine our confidence in our identity in **Christ**. **"And I heard a loud voice saying in heaven, Now is come salvation, and strength, and the kingdom of our God, and the power of his Christ: for the accuser of our brethren is cast down, which accused them before our God day and night." (Revelation 12:10 KJV).** The enemy may use tactics such as suppression, oppression, or even depression to deviate us from our path. Yet, the Christian's stance is not built upon the shaky grounds of repression but on the solid rock of confession.

In **Numbers 11:6**, the Israelites remembered the food in Egypt and felt a lack, forgetting the provision of **God**. They said, **"But now our soul is dried away: there is nothing at all, beside this manna, before our eyes." Similarly, when we hold onto unconfessed sins or suppress our wrongdoings, it's akin to holding onto stale manna. In time, it will curdle within us, leading to spiritual decay. Confession brings forth liberation. "If we confess our sins, he is faithful and just to forgive us our sins, and to cleanse us from all unrighteousness." (1 John 1:9 KJV)**

God's desire is for us to transition from our metaphorical Egypt – a place of bondage – to our Canaan, a land of promise and abundance. **"For I know the plans I have for you, declares the LORD, plans for welfare and not for evil, to give you a future and a hope." (Jeremiah 29:11 KJV).** This transition, however, is activated by faith. The essence of faith is beautifully captured in **Hebrews 11:1 KJV, "Now faith is the substance of things hoped for, the evidence of things not seen."**

The duality of faith and fear is evident. While faith attracts blessings, fear draws negativity. As children of **God**, we operate in faith, making us magnets for **God's** blessings. **"For the LORD God is a sun and shield: the LORD will give grace and glory: no good thing will he withhold from them that walk uprightly." (Psalm 84:11 KJV).** This promise aligns with **God's** intention to give us **His** kingdom, as proclaimed in **Luke 12:32 KJV, "Fear not, little flock; for it is your Father's good pleasure to give you the kingdom."**

In, as **God's Mighty Men**, our lives should resonate with faith and confidence. This does not only pertain to our spiritual journey but encompasses all facets of our lives, from our businesses and marriages to our recreational pursuits. By anchoring ourselves in **God's** promises and walking in faith, we can experience the fullness of **God's** kingdom here on earth, proving that we truly are **God's Mighty Men**, endowed with strength and purpose for such a time as this.

CHAPTER NINE

The Power of Obedience in Action

The Bible has a tapestry of tales about the faith and acts of **Mighty Men** and women of **God**. These individuals were not just **Mighty** because of their physical strength or intellectual prowess but because of their unwavering obedience to the commands of **God**.

"And Samuel said, Hath the Lord as great delight in burnt offerings and sacrifices, as in obeying the voice of the Lord? Behold, to obey is better than sacrifice, and to hearken than the fat of rams." - 1 Samuel 15:22 (KJV)

This scripture resonates with the essential message that obedience is paramount in the life of a believer. The divine directive for our lives can be mystifying. Many times, we find ourselves in the dilemma of discerning **God's** will. Yet, the roadmap to the realization of **His** will is simple: unwavering obedience.

The most profound spiritual accomplishments do not emerge from sheer strength or skill but from an unyielding commitment to do the **Lord**'s bidding. It isn't about the magnitude of the task but the magnitude of the obedience that accompanies it.

"If ye love me, keep my commandments." - John 14:15 (KJV)

God's favor and power do not rest upon those who merely offer lip service or ceremonial acts. It is not about ritualistic acts or trying to manipulate the heavens to descend with power. It is the simple acts of obedience, like sweeping the floor when told to, that release **God's** anointing upon a life.

Recall the story of the widow at Zarephath. The Prophet Elijah asked her for a morsel of bread. Despite her limited resources, she obeyed, and as a result, her oil and flour did not run out. It wasn't about the bread or the oil but her obedience to **God's** prophet.

"And the barrel of meal wasted not, neither did the cruse of oil fail, according to the word of the LORD, which he spake by Elijah." - 1 Kings 17:16 (KJV)

In today's discourse, many seek **God's** power. They want the ability to heal, prophesy, and perform wonders. But without a foundation of obedience, these pursuits are futile. For **God** does not seek the **Mighty** in strength but the **Mighty** in obedience.

In the end, it is imperative to understand that the journey of faith is punctuated by acts of obedience, both great and small. These acts are not just tasks but testimonies, not just deeds but declarations of our commitment to **God's** will.

In, **God's Mighty Men** are not determined by the worldly standards of might but by the spiritual standard of obedience. From the smallest act like sweeping a floor to the monumental challenge of raising the dead, power is released not because of the magnitude of the act but the magnitude of obedience behind it. As we walk in this journey of faith, let us remember to prioritize obedience above all else, for therein lies the true power and favor of **God**. Amen.

God's Mighty Men in Spirit and Action"

In the Christian walk, understanding the will and power of **God** is paramount. When **Christ** articulated, **"If ye love me, keep my commandments" (John 14:15, KJV), He** wasn't merely advocating for blind obedience but was emphasizing the profound relationship between knowing and doing **God's** will. **Jesus** asserts, **"If a man love me, he will keep my words: and my Father will love him, and we will come unto him, and make our abode with him" (John 14:23, KJV).** This illustrates that to know the power of **God**, one must first align themselves with **His** will.

The spiritual journey from Egypt to Canaan is a prominent example of this. As depicted in the scriptures, **God** delivered the Israelites from the clutches of Pharaoh, symbolizing worldly bondage, and led them towards the Promised Land, Canaan. This journey symbolizes a believer's transition from a life immersed in worldly desires to a life dedicated to divine pursuits. However, as the scripture narrates, **"Wherefore come out from among them, and be ye separate, saith the Lord" (2 Corinthians 6:17, KJV)**, it's imperative to discern that mere separation from the world isn't enough. One must also be separated unto **God**, cementing their identification with **Him.**

There's an inherent power in our identification with **God**. This is not merely a separation from worldly desires, but a strong alignment with **God's** purpose. The Holy Ghost has bestowed upon believers the gift of speech to advocate for **Him,** for **"For the kingdom of God is not in word, but in power" (1 Corinthians 4:20, KJV).** To be silent in the face of worldly opposition or temptation is to give the world an upper hand. Yet, by boldly professing our faith, identifying with **Christ**, and speaking **His** word, believers offer **Christ** an advantage, asserting **His** dominion over worldly challenges.

This concept of silence reminds us of the age-old adage: Sometimes, silence is golden, but at other times, it is indicative of fear or complacency. This passive silence can be detrimental to a believer's spiritual walk. As mentioned in Proverbs**, "The wicked flee when no man pursueth: but the righteous are bold as a lion" (Proverbs 28:1, KJV).** Our identification with **Christ** ought to embolden us, making us **Mighty Men** and women of **God**.

Engaging actively with fellow believers, encouraging them in their walk, and acknowledging their divine identity plays a pivotal role in strengthening our community. By recognizing and affirming one another's identity in **Christ**, we fortify our collective resolve to serve **God**.

The journey of spiritual growth is intrinsically linked to our identification with **God**. As believers, it's not enough to merely separate ourselves from the world; we must also ardently embrace our identity in **Christ**. Through this dual process of separation and identification, we become **Mighty Men** and women of **God**, equipped and empowered to manifest **His** will on Earth. In this journey, our boldness, derived from our alignment with **God's** purpose, serves as our shield, ensuring we remain steadfast in our commitment to **Him.**

Identification with the Divine

Throughout human history, there have been powerful testimonies of individuals who dared to identify with a force larger than themselves, especially the divine power of **Jesus Christ**. These individuals, often referred to as "**God's Mighty Men**," chose to merge their identity with that of **Jesus**, reflecting a profound spiritual relationship. Their dedication showcases the essence of what it means to be fully surrendered and identified with the Savior.

The Gospels are rife with the teachings of **Jesus Christ**, guiding us on the path of righteousness. In the book of Matthew, **Jesus** articulately states: **"For whosoever will**

save his life shall lose it: and whosoever will lose his life for my sake shall find it." (Matthew 16:25, KJV). This teaching, profound in its implications, demands a deep introspection. It is not about the physical act of losing one's life but signifies a spiritual surrender, an absolute identification with **Jesus**, and a disidentification from worldly desires and egos.

When we profess our faith, declare **Jesus Christ** as our savior, and align our identities with **Him,** we embark on a spiritual journey of transformation. We become "**God's Mighty Men**," losing our worldly identity to gain a spiritual one. As written in the book of Romans: **"That if thou shalt confess with thy mouth the Lord Jesus, and shalt believe in thine heart that God hath raised him from the dead, thou shalt be saved." (Romans 10:9, KJV).** This confession is an act of bravery, an affirmation of faith, and a testament to our spiritual identity.

The beautiful paradox of the gospel is that in losing ourselves, we find an identity greater than any worldly title or honor. Just as when we put our trust in the name of **Jesus**, we transition from a earthly title to a heavenly identity. It's a humble act, transcending our mortal understanding, becoming one with the eternal.

To not confess **Jesus**, to not identify with Him is to attempt to save our own lives based on our own understanding, leading to an eventual loss. As **Jesus** said, **"Whosoever therefore shall be ashamed of me and of my words in this adulterous and sinful generation; of him also shall the Son of man be ashamed, when he**

cometh in the glory of his Father with the holy angels." (Mark 8:38, KJV).

To raise our hands and identify with **Jesus**, to openly and boldly confess Him as our **Lord** and Savior, is to align ourselves with eternal life. This act of faith and surrender resonates with the words from the book of John: **"But as many as received him, to them gave he power to become the sons of God, even to them that believe on his name." (John 1:12, KJV).** The very thought that **Jesus** allows us, mere mortals, to identify with Him is a testament to **His** profound love and grace. The greater wonder, however, lies in the fact that **He**, the King of Kings, would desire to identify with us.

The journey of "**God's Mighty Men**" is one of profound transformation, from worldly identification to a spiritual alignment with **Jesus Christ**. It's a testament to the divine love, grace, and mercy bestowed upon us. Identifying with **Jesus** is not just about losing our earthly identities but gaining an eternal one. In doing so, we experience the profound love and grace that comes from being one with the Savior. And in this spiritual symbiosis, the most profound revelation is not just our identification with **Jesus**, but **His** identification with us. Hallelujah!

Exploration of Spiritual Vigor in the Light of Scriptures

The Bible, with its countless testimonies, heroes of faith, and promises, frequently points to the potential in each believer. Among the various figures and narratives in this sacred book, there is an underlying theme of the **Mighty Men** of **God** who displayed unwavering faith and courage in their walk with the Almighty. Through their stories, we can decipher crucial life lessons and insights into what it means to be identified with **Christ**.

The essence of a believer's journey is to realize their spiritual identity. **"God is not ashamed to be called their God" (Hebrews 11:16, KJV).** The same **God** who took glory in the patriarchs, the prophets, and the disciples takes glory in you. When one receives the anointing of the Holy Ghost, it is an affirmation of this celestial bond. As the Apostle Paul reminds us in Ephesians, **"In whom ye also trusted, after that ye heard the word of truth, the gospel of your salvation: in whom also after that ye believed, ye were sealed with that Holy Spirit of promise," (Ephesians 1:13, KJV).** Such anointing is not just a sign but an affirmation of **God's** association and identification with us.

However, this identity doesn't come without its challenges. Often believers find themselves in the wilderness of spiritual stagnation. The metaphor of being "half-baked" can be likened to the lukewarm Christian life described in Revelation: **"So then because thou art lukewarm, and neither cold nor hot, I will spue thee out of my mouth" (Revelation 3:16, KJV).** Straddling between the kingdom of **God** and the desires of the world invariably leads to pain and loss. To be identified with

Jesus, one needs to be wholeheartedly committed to **Him.**

Among the challenges that thwart a man's spiritual progress is lust. This isn't just the lust associated with illicit desires but a deeper longing that deviates from the path of righteousness. Scriptures warn about lust in multiple places, notably in James: **"But every man is tempted, when he is drawn away of his own lust, and enticed. Then when lust hath conceived, it bringeth forth sin: and sin, when it is finished, bringeth forth death" (James 1:14-15, KJV).** The struggle against lust, among other sins, is real. Yet, it's essential to understand that the nature of **God's** kingdom is positive, and by focusing on the positive characteristics emanating from the character of the King, believers can overcome these challenges.

Furthermore, understanding the characteristics of the kingdom leads one to live a life filled with the fruits of the Spirit. **"But the fruit of the Spirit is love, joy, peace, longsuffering, gentleness, goodness, faith, Meekness, temperance: against such there is no law" (Galatians 5:22-23, KJV).** These fruits are the manifestation of a life fully identified with **Christ**, a life that emanates positivity in the face of worldly temptations.

To be counted among **God's Mighty Men** requires understanding our identity in **Christ**, recognizing the challenges we face in our spiritual journey, and committing to the characteristics of **His** kingdom. By continually immersing ourselves in the Word, seeking the anointing of the Holy Ghost, and striving to live in the positive realm of the Spirit, we can walk in the path of those heroes of faith, fully identified with our Savior, **Jesus Christ**.

A Deep Dive into the Essence of Divine Faith

In our spiritual journey, it is paramount that we recognize and internalize the divine essence of faith. It is the powerful testament of our unbreakable bond with **God**. Our lives are filled with trials and tribulations, joys and sorrows. But throughout this roller coaster, there's an underlying theme that remains unchanged: the ever-prevailing spirit of **God's Mighty Men** and women. When we speak of **God's Mighty** individuals, we do not refer to those with physical strength, but more profoundly, those with indomitable spiritual stamina and unwavering faith.

"And without faith it is impossible to please him: for he that cometh to God must believe that he is, and that he is a rewarder of them that diligently seek him." - Hebrews 11:6 (KJV)

It is vital to deeply ingrain in our minds and spirits the undeniable power of **God's** words. These words are the guiding light, the north star in our darkest nights, and the soothing balm in our most harrowing pains. They serve as a testament to **God's** never-ending love and faith in us. The spiritual encounter is not just an event but a lifelong experience that should be imprinted on our minds and hearts.

The divine nature of these words and experiences ensures that they come to the forefront of our memories in times of need. These are not mere utterances of a human being, but the timeless wisdom of the Almighty. We are urged to look beyond the person conveying the message and focus on the essence of the message itself.

"Thy word have I hid in mine heart, that I might not sin against thee." - Psalms 119:11 (KJV)

In **God's** kingdom, the essence of love is unparalleled. It is not the worldly love that we are so accustomed to but a love that is eternal, selfless, and devoid of any expectations. This love can only be comprehended, cherished, and reciprocated if we truly understand its origin.

"Beloved, let us love one another: for love is of God; and every one that loveth is born of God, and knoweth God." - 1 John 4:7 (KJV)

It is crucial to understand that the faith in our hearts, which assures us of our salvation, is not ours but that of **Jesus Christ**, who lives within us. While our faith may waver or falter, the divine faith gifted to us remains steadfast. The disciples' query about faith reinforces the idea that even a minuscule amount of this divine faith has the potency to move mountains and assure salvation.

"And Jesus said unto them, Because of your unbelief: for verily I say unto you, If ye have faith as a grain of

mustard seed, ye shall say unto this mountain, Remove hence to yonder place; and it shall remove; and nothing shall be impossible unto you." - Matthew 17:20 (KJV)

God's Mighty Men and women are not just warriors in the battlefield but warriors of faith. They are armed with an indomitable spirit, unwavering faith, and a heart full of **God's** love. As we journey through life, it is these attributes that will light our path, shield us from despair, and lead us to salvation. The essence of divine faith is the beacon that ensures we are never lost, for even in our darkest moments, the light of the **Lord** shines the brightest. Remember, it is not the quantity but the quality of our faith that determines our spiritual strength. And with even a mustard seed of this divine faith, we are equipped to overcome any challenge and achieve spiritual enlightenment.

The Power of Divine Faith in the Lives of Believers

The journey of faith is one that resonates with countless individuals throughout history, binding us together through shared experiences and understanding. Yet, the nature of faith and how it manifests in our lives remains a subject of deep contemplation and reflection. Throughout the scriptures, the distinction between human faith and divine faith is evident. One could even argue that understanding this distinction is the key to unlocking a profound relationship with the Divine.

"That's all you got to have. But you can have a barn full of human faith and never be saved. Human faith has doubt built into it. Divine faith has no doubt." This repetition emphasizes a point that is fundamental in our spiritual journey. As stated in **Hebrews 11:1 (KJV): "Now faith is the substance of things hoped for, the evidence of things not seen."** Divine faith transcends our human limitations, taking us beyond mere belief into the realm of unquestionable assurance.

The faith we possess after salvation is not born of our flesh or human intellect. Instead, it originates from the Divine, granted to us through the indwelling spirit of **Jesus**. **Galatians 2:20 (KJV)** reinforces this truth, saying, **"I am crucified with Christ: nevertheless I live; yet not I, but Christ liveth in me: and the life which I now live in the flesh I live by the faith of the Son of God, who loved me, and gave himself for me."**

When believers claim to love **God**, this affection isn't merely a human emotion but the very love **Jesus** holds for the Father. This divine love is made manifest within us through the indwelling of **His** spirit. **Romans 5:5 (KJV)** beautifully captures this: **"And hope maketh not ashamed; because the love of God is shed abroad in our hearts by the Holy Ghost which is given unto us."**

As stewards of this faith and love, believers are called to feed on the Word of **God**. It is through the scriptures that our faith grows and the anointing of the Spirit strengthens our bond with the Divine. This relationship transforms our very beings, enabling us to think **His** thoughts, feel **His** feelings, speak **His** words, and perform **His** works.

The levels of faith that believer's journey through evolve from the recognition that **God** is for us to the realization that **God** is with us, and in us. The pinnacle of this spiritual ascent lies in the last truth, acknowledging and experiencing that **God** is within us. The Apostle Paul's assertion in **Colossians 1:27 (KJV)** underscores this truth: **"To whom God would make known what is the riches of the glory of this mystery among the Gentiles; which is Christ in you, the hope of glory."**

To be chosen by **God** to serve as a vessel, through which **He** reveals **His Mighty** power, is a privilege like no other. Those who have experienced this know the overwhelming awe that envelops them when they witness **His** words flowing through them, often leaving them in wonder.

The journey of faith, marked by the transition from human to divine faith, is not just an individual's spiritual evolution but a testament to **God's** unyielding love and desire to work within and through us. In understanding this profound relationship, believers find themselves not only drawn closer to the Divine but also endowed with the power to influence the world in **His** name. As the chosen vessels of **God's** love and power, we are beckoned to rise to the highest level of faith, ensuring that **His** glory shines through every word spoken and every deed done.

The Spiritual Identification with Christ

In our world today, there is a plethora of distractions and temptations that seem to pull us away from our spiritual path. When we encounter situations that do not align with our spiritual values, our spirits are often grieved. Walking past a place that symbolizes a low level of life or observing content that is against our moral beliefs can be deeply disturbing.

"And have no fellowship with the unfruitful works of darkness, but rather reprove them. For it is a shame even to speak of those things which are done of them in secret." (Ephesians 5:11-12 KJV)

But have you ever noticed that there are times when certain things didn't bother you? But now they do. This change in perception and emotional response is not because of any personal growth, but because of the Holy Spirit dwelling within us. When we are grieved by the wrong things in the world, it is the Holy Spirit within us that is grieved.

"And grieve not the holy Spirit of God, whereby ye are sealed unto the day of redemption." (Ephesians 4:30 KJV)

When we speak words of righteousness and **Godliness**, it's not us, but the spirit of **Jesus** speaking through us. This is a profound realization that we, as believers, are so identified with **Jesus** that we start to think **His** thoughts, feel **His** feelings, and act according to **His** will.

"For as many as are led by the Spirit of God, they are the sons of God." (Romans 8:14 KJV)

This identification with **Christ** is a deep spiritual mystery, a union so intimate that we become conduits of **His** power and love in the world. This is why, when faced with situations to heal or bless others, we shouldn't doubt our abilities or faith. It's not about our strength or faith but **His**. If **Jesus** were present, would **He** heal? Would **He** bless? Would **He** speak words of life? The answer is a resounding YES. And since **He** lives within us, we should do the same.

"Verily, verily, I say unto you, He that believeth on me, the works that I do shall he do also; and greater works than these shall he do; because I go unto my Father." (John 14:12 KJV)

Therefore, when faced with doubt or fear, remember it's not about our limited human faith. We are called to operate in **His** boundless faith, for **His** spirit is within us.

"But the fruit of the Spirit is love, joy, peace, longsuffering, gentleness, goodness, faith," (Galatians 5:22 KJV)

Our journey as believers is not just about our personal growth but about our identification with **Christ**. As we grow closer to **Him,** we become more like **Him.** This process is not just about avoiding sin or doing good deeds, but about allowing the Holy Spirit to transform us from the inside out. As **God's Mighty Men**, let's continue to seek a deeper relationship with **Jesus**, letting **His** thoughts, feelings, words, and works shine through us, bearing witness to **His** great love and power in our world.

A Study on Love, Law, and Divine Anointing

"Faith cometh by hearing, and hearing by the word of God." (Romans 10:17, KJV)

Every congregation should erupt in praise, clapping not out of mere formality but for a cause, for a being, for the very person of **Jesus Christ**. This clapping, echoing loudly, symbolizes the church's connection, their deep-seated faith in the Savior.

The Glory of Jesus

Everything in the realm of Christianity points back to **Jesus**. **He** is the foundation, the chief cornerstone, the glory, the power, and the entirety of the church's purpose. Christians find their identity in **Jesus Christ**. As it is written, **"For in him we live, and move, and have our being." (Acts 17:28, KJV)**

An Anointing of Passion

It is not out of mere emotion or enthusiasm that we rejoice and get excited about our **Lord** and Savior. It is the anointing of the Holy Spirit, a divine power that fuels this fiery passion. This anointing transcends beyond the preacher, touching every soul present, promising change and renewal. **God** is in the business of transforming lives, redefining destinies, and filling hearts with **His** love.

The Essence of Divine Love

The scripture declares, **"For God so loved the world, that he gave his only begotten Son, that whosoever believeth in him should not perish, but have everlasting life." (John 3:16, KJV)** This love is a sacrificial love. It seeks to benefit others at its own expense. Love is about giving, not receiving. When love is in action, it is selfless, always seeking the best for others. Such love is a reflection of **God's** nature, for **God** is love (1 John 4:8, KJV).

Contrasting Love with Its Opposite

While emotionally, hate stands against love, legally, it's the law that contrasts with love. An environment filled with love naturally abides by principles of respect and care. But where love diminishes, rules and regulations surge, filling the void, enforcing what should naturally flow from the heart. The statement, "Little love, much law; much love, little law," resonates with this truth. It reminds us of **Jesus**'s words: **"A new commandment I give unto you, That ye love one another; as I have loved you, that ye also love one another." (John 13:34, KJV)**

A Word for Ministers

The peculiarities and tendencies of preachers have been

noted. Often, while preaching about laws and regulations, they tend to practice grace. This highlights a crucial aspect of the Christian walk. It's not about the dos and don'ts but about embodying the love and grace of **Jesus Christ**.

God's Mighty Men are those who recognize the importance of love, understand the place of the law, and operate under the anointing of the Holy Spirit. They champion faith, uphold the glory of **Jesus**, and spread **His** love unconditionally. In a world in need of hope, these **Mighty Men**, fueled by love and grace, shine as beacons of light, pointing all towards the Savior. May every believer strive to be such a vessel, for in doing so, we truly become the hands and feet of **Christ** on Earth.

A Spiritual Examination

Spiritual journeys and growth paths are inherently unique. They are as diverse as the colors of a rainbow, and trying to fit them into a predetermined mold could lead to diminished vitality and authenticity.

The foundation of our belief is grounded in the Holy Bible. As we look into the scriptures, we are reminded in **Romans 14:4 (KJV), "Who art thou that judgest another man's servant? To his own master he standeth or falleth. Yea, he shall be holden up: for God is able to make him stand."** This reinforces the idea that our personal convictions and connections with

God are deeply personal and should not be judged by fellow believers.

When one attempts to enforce their own spiritual convictions onto others, it can lead to the stifling of genuine spiritual growth. This notion is metaphorically depicted as producing "Lukewarm Christians" when we try to mold everyone to our own pattern of consecration. This approach can be particularly dangerous when applied to young, impressionable minds. **Proverbs 22:6 (KJV)** advises, **"Train up a child in the way he should go: and when he is old, he will not depart from it."** Yet, this training should be rooted in understanding, wisdom, and individuality rather than conformity.

The convictions and consecrations one individual experiences should not be imposed as a blanket rule upon a congregation. As the Apostle Paul mentions in **1 Corinthians 10:29 (KJV), "For why is my liberty judged of another man's conscience?"** Everyone should be allowed the freedom to interact with **God** based on their unique relationship and understanding.

Psalm 139:14 (KJV), "I will praise thee; for I am fearfully and wonderfully made: marvellous are thy works; and that my soul knoweth right well."

In our journey to understand and embrace **God's** might, we must remember that spiritual growth is inherently personal. While guidance from leaders and mentors can be invaluable, it's essential to nurture and encourage individual relationships with **God**. We must resist the temptation to impose our convictions on others, understanding that **God** has created each of us uniquely. In doing so, we not only honor the diverse tapestry of faith but also ensure that our spiritual community remains vibrant, genuine, and ever-evolving in its relationship with the Divine.

Walking in Spiritual Authority

"For by grace are ye saved through faith; and that not of yourselves: it is the gift of God." (Ephesians 2:8, KJV)

The story of the Bible is one of redemption, grace, and **God's** unending love for mankind. As believers in **Christ**, we recognize that our standing with **God** is not achieved through works or human efforts but is rather a divine act of grace. But who are **God's Mighty Men**? And how do they serve as exemplars of spiritual strength and authority?

The term '**Mighty Men**' harks back to the Old Testament, where King David had a band of elite warriors who performed feats of incredible bravery. They were not just physical warriors; their allegiance and trust in **God** made them spiritual warriors as well. In the context of 2 Samuel 23:8-39, we read of their remarkable exploits that inspired the entire nation of Israel.

As believers, we can draw parallels between these **Mighty Men** and the spiritual warriors of today. Those who stand firm in their faith, those who declare the Word of **God** with boldness, and those who are unashamed of the Gospel of **Christ**.

The spiritual statements we confess over our lives have power. **Proverbs 18:21 (KJV) says, "Death and life are in the power of the tongue: and they that love it shall eat the fruit thereof."** When we identify with **Jesus Christ** in word, blood, and spirit, we are making a powerful proclamation.

"But as many as received him, to them gave he power to become the sons of God, even to them that believe on his name." (John 1:12, KJV)

This declaration resonates with the love of **God** that has been poured into our hearts. Paul writes in **Romans 5:5 (KJV), "And hope maketh not ashamed; because the love of God is shed abroad in our hearts by the Holy Ghost which is given unto us."**

Our love for our brethren, the church, our pastors, and the Word of **God** is a testament to the transformative power of the Holy Spirit in us. The anointing we carry is not just for ourselves, but to be a blessing to others, to be **God's Mighty Men** and women in this generation.

In, **God's Mighty Men** are not just figures of the past but are reflective of every believer who walks in spiritual authority today. By the grace of **God**, we have been brought into a life of love, commitment, and divine purpose. As we stand firm in our identity in **Christ** and continue to walk in love, we too can be counted among

God's Mighty Men, making an impact for the Kingdom of **God**.

"And they overcame him by the blood of the Lamb, and by the word of their testimony; and they loved not their lives unto the death." (Revelation 12:11, KJV)

Love, Law, and Lust in the Two Kingdoms

"For the kingdom of God is not meat and drink; but righteousness, and peace, and joy in the Holy Ghost." - Romans 14:17 (KJV)

In our journey of faith, understanding the nuances of the kingdoms that confront us is paramount. In the tapestry of life, we encounter two primary kingdoms - the kingdom of **God** and the kingdom of Satan.

The kingdom of **God** is characterized by righteousness, peace, and joy. It is everything that echoes positivity, growth, and love. **"And now abideth faith, hope, love, these three; but the greatest of these is love." - 1 Corinthians 13:13 (KJV).** Here, love reigns supreme, signaling a desire to benefit others, often at personal expense. This love is foundational, emanating from the very nature of the King Himself.

Contrarily, the kingdom of Satan represents what **God** never intended for humanity. It's built on negatives, and unbelief, distancing us from the original purpose and the blessings of Canaan land. Separation from this kingdom isn't the sole objective; we ought to be wholly separated, setting our hearts on **God's** promises.

Our identities in **Gods** kingdom is defined tri-fold: by the **Word**, by **blood**, and by our **identification** with **Jesus Christ**. **"In whom we have redemption through his blood, even the forgiveness of sins" - Colossians 1:14 (KJV).** If we lose our life, it's through our alliance with **Jesus**. This bond with **Christ** is cemented by our confession of faith.

Understanding why the children of Israel failed to enter Canaan provides us insights into the pitfalls we must avoid. Lust is the first deterrent. While love is the hallmark of **God's** kingdom, lust epitomizes Satan's dominion. Love gives selflessly, but lust seeks to gain, often at the detriment of others. Love and lust are diametrically opposed in their core intent. **"For all that is in the world, the lust of the flesh, and the lust of the eyes, and the pride of life, is not of the Father, but is of the world." - 1 John 2:16 (KJV).**

This dichotomy extends beyond mere emotion. Legally, where love offers grace, the opposite facet operates on stringent laws. Morally, where love values the collective good, its counterpart, lust, promotes self-centeredness. The governance of these two kingdoms varies. In **God's** realm, **Jesus Christ** is the **Lord**. In Satan's territory, self is exalted.

Thus, it's essential to internalize this profound truth:

"Much love, little law; little love, much law." When love flourishes, the need for laws diminishes, and vice versa. A society or individual consumed by self-interest, symbolized by the 'I' in SIN, strays from **God's** path, shackling themselves with man-made laws.

The eternal struggle between the two kingdoms isn't just an external battle but an internal one. As believers, our challenge is to recognize these kingdoms within us, choose love over lust, grace over law, and **Jesus Christ** over self. It is in making this choice that we truly become **God's Mighty Men**, standing firm in faith and purpose.

"Ye are of God, little children, and have overcome them: because greater is he that is in you, than he that is in the world." - 1 John 4:4 (KJV).

Overcoming Sin and Lust

"The heart is deceitful above all things, and desperately wicked: who can know it?" - Jeremiah 17:9 (KJV).

Sin, seems to revolve around a singular, self-centered nucleus: "I". The essence of sin, at its core, is fundamentally linked to self. This profound realization transcends mere observation, moving into the domain of profound spiritual introspection.

"In the beginning was the Word, and the Word was

with God, and the Word was God." - John 1:1 (KJV). The Scriptures teach us that it wasn't the literal apple from the orchard that initiated sin, but rather, it was the inclination of the heart that committed the act. The heart, a realm of desires, choices, and inclinations, became susceptible to the deception of self, leading mankind away from **God's** ideal.

For what is sin but the overwhelming impulse to serve oneself at the expense of others? When viewed through this lens, lust emerges as a manifestation of this sin. Lust, in its raw form, is the aspiration to satisfy oneself, sidelining **God's** intentions and design.

"From whence come wars and fightings among you? come they not hence, even of your lusts that war in your members?" - James 4:1 (KJV). Nations, corporations, dictators, and individuals alike can all fall prey to this consuming fire of lust. A government, motivated by lust, disregards the well-being of its citizens, seeing them as mere tools for achieving selfish ambitions. Similarly, a corporation driven by unchecked lust may forsake the welfare of its employees or the satisfaction of its customers.

Tragically, this insidious form of self-gratification isn't limited to abstract entities. It finds its place in the intimate relationships between men and women. The deceptive flattery, the pretense of love, and the eventual betrayal bear testimony to a heart driven by lust and not genuine love. **"For where envying and strife is, there is confusion and every evil work." - James 3:16 (KJV).**

Indeed, in the sacred bond of marriage, a man can fall into the trap of lusting after his wife. The Scriptures say, **"Marriage is honourable in all, and the bed undefiled: but whoremongers and adulterers God will judge." - Hebrews 13:4 (KJV).** The sanctity of this union can be defiled if one's heart is not in the right place, emphasizing the importance of maintaining purity even within the marital bed.

In , it is vital for **God's Mighty Men** to be vigilant, discerning, and grounded in the Word. The battle against sin and lust begins in the heart. By turning our eyes upon **Jesus**, immersing ourselves in **His** Word, and seeking daily renewal, we can indeed rise above the 'I' in sin and strive towards righteousness. **"I can do all things through Christ which strengtheneth me." - Philippians 4:13 (KJV).**

The Spiritual War Within

"Dearly beloved, I beseech you as strangers and pilgrims, abstain from fleshly lusts, which war against the soul;" (1 Peter 2:11, KJV)

The struggle of humanity with fleshly desires is as ancient as the Biblical narratives themselves. From Adam's misstep in the Garden of Eden to King David's sinful encounter with Bathsheba, the Scriptures are replete with accounts of **Mighty Men** of **God** battling the insidious lure of temptation. But what differentiates the **Mighty** from the fallen is their approach to these temptations and the spiritual fortitude they maintain.

1. The Misunderstood Concept of Love and Lust

When a man looks at a woman, there's a thin line between admiration and lust. While admiration respects the sanctity of another's existence, lust seeks to objectify and dominate. Lust reduces a person to an object, an idea, or a fantasy.

"Ye have heard that it was said by them of old time, Thou shalt not commit adultery: But I say unto you, That whosoever looketh on a woman to lust after her hath committed adultery with her already in his heart." (Matthew 5:27-28, KJV)

This scripture from the Book of Matthew underscores the spiritual implications of lustful intent. In the act of fantasizing, one distances themselves from their partner and establishes a spiritual chasm.

2. The Spiritual Dimensions of Intimacy

Marital intimacy is not just a physical act, but a profound spiritual communion between two souls. In the throes of intimacy, couples communicate not just with words and gestures but also spiritually. If the mind wanders into the realms of fantasy, the spirit senses that deceit. Such transgressions cause feelings of betrayal and disappointment.

3. The Idolatry of Pornography and Fantasies

The Bible warns us against the dangers of idolatry. Pornography, with its illusory depictions, becomes a tool of idolatry. It offers a skewed representation of intimacy, creating images and strongholds in the mind.

"For they have committed adultery, and blood is in their hands, and with their idols have they committed adultery…" (Ezekiel 23:37, KJV)

Habitual acts driven by these fantasies become nothing short of worshipping these false idols. Such behavior distances individuals from their partners, creating an environment where true love and intimacy cannot flourish.

4. Breaking Free from the Strongholds

To liberate oneself from the chains of these fantasies, one must recognize and cast them down as the idols they are. The Biblical call to repentance is a reminder of **God's** infinite mercy and the promise of redemption.

"If we confess our sins, he is faithful and just to forgive us our sins, and to cleanse us from all unrighteousness." (1 John 1:9, KJV)

The battles within our minds can often be the most daunting. However, through spiritual strength, the guidance of Scriptures, and a genuine love for our partners, we can overcome these challenges. **Mighty Men** of **God** are not defined by an absence of temptation but by their resilience and determination to pursue righteousness. The journey towards spiritual purity requires constant introspection, confession, and an unwavering commitment to the Word of **God**.

CHAPTER TEN

Battling Lust, Idolatry, and Temptations with Faith

In our human experience, one of the most profound challenges we face is the battle against our own desires. The Bible provides us with guidance on these challenges, teaching us to navigate our impulses with wisdom and grace. This discourse seeks to explore the issues of lust, idolatry, and various temptations, highlighting the spiritual weapons available to **God's Mighty Men** and women.

The mention of "lust" often brings to mind images of sexual desire, but lust extends far beyond this narrow definition. In essence, lust can be seen as an overpowering desire or craving, which can manifest in numerous ways. Financially, it might be the urge to amass wealth at the expense of others. Familiarly, it might manifest as imposing one's own desires upon others to an unhealthy degree. The Bible warns us against such overpowering desires in **James 4:1-2 (KJV): "From whence come wars and fightings among you? come they not hence, even of your lusts that war in your members? Ye lust, and have not: ye kill, and desire to have, and cannot obtain: ye fight and war, yet ye have not, because ye ask not."**

Lust can also extend into our relationships and marital

bonds. When acts of seeming generosity are veiled attempts to control or dominate, this too can be seen as a form of lust. One must be careful to not be consumed by worldly desires, or as **1 John 2:16 (KJV)** puts it: **"For all that is in the world, the lust of the flesh, and the lust of the eyes, and the pride of life, is not of the Father, but is of the world."**

God's desire for us is clear: to break free from the chains of lust and to find our purpose and satisfaction in **Him.** This involves recognizing our vulnerabilities and confronting them head-on, allowing **Christ** to work within us to overcome. The New Testament offers encouragement in this regard. As **Romans 8:1-2 (KJV)** declares, **"There is therefore now no condemnation to them which are in Christ Jesus, who walk not after the flesh, but after the Spirit. For the law of the Spirit of life in Christ Jesus hath made me free from the law of sin and death."**

Another perilous trap is idolatry. Idolatry is not just the worship of graven images; it extends to anything that takes precedence over our devotion to **God**. This could be our job, our hobbies, or even our ministries. The first commandment is clear in **Exodus 20:3 (KJV): "Thou shalt have no other Gods before me."** To prioritize anything over **God** is to challenge **His** rightful place in our lives. Our Creator yearns for our full devotion, a relationship untainted by the distractions of worldly idols.

Tempting **Christ**, or demanding that **God** acts contrary to **His** nature, is another area of caution. This is exemplified in **Matthew 4:7 (KJV)** where **Jesus** responds to Satan's temptation: **"Jesus said unto him, It is written again, Thou shalt not tempt the Lord thy God."**

Lastly, murmuring, or persistent complaining, can erode our faith. **Philippians 2:14 (KJV)** advises, **"Do all things without murmurings and disputings."**

In this journey of faith, it is essential to recognize the obstacles that might divert our path. Whether it be lust, idolatry, or any other temptation, we must remain vigilant and anchored in the Word of **God**. As **God's Mighty Men** and women, we have the spiritual tools and teachings to overcome, ensuring that our devotion remains steadfast and our spirit unyielding. With the grace of **God**, every challenge can be surmounted, every temptation resisted, leading us ever closer to our Creator.

Embracing the Principle of Giving Time, Talent, and Treasure

Murmuring – the constant act of complaining or grumbling – is more than just an external expression of discontent. It signifies a deeper misalignment with spiritual priorities. Often, the act of murmuring distracts us from our genuine responsibilities and devotions to **God**, leading us to forget **His** divine sovereignty over time and provision.

Paul, in the book of Corinthians, states: **"Do all things**

without murmurings and disputings" (Philippians 2:14, KJV). This directive emphasizes the need for a faithful heart that operates without complaint, recognizing **God's** grace and plan.

Many modern believers often misunderstand the concept of giving **God** the first day of the week. Sunday, the **Lord**'s Day, symbolizes more than just a day to worship; it represents a dedication of our week to **God**. The New Testament encourages us to live by faith, not by sight: **"For we walk by faith, not by sight" (2 Corinthians 5:7, KJV).** This means that when we devote our Sundays wholly to **God**, trusting in **Him,** we can expect blessings and provisions for the rest of the week.

The biblical principle of giving isn't limited to financial giving. While most associate giving with money, the broader principle encourages the giving of one's time, talent, and treasure. Imagine a church where every member utilized their unique talents for **God's** work! The growth would be unprecedented. Many professionals have already begun this journey, donating their skills and expertise to serve the less fortunate, exemplifying the power of giving talent.

If every believer embraced this principle, the societal impact would be monumental. Welfare systems could be overhauled, and communities transformed. All it takes is for each of us to recognize the power of giving our talent and time for the greater good.

By giving our time, talent, and treasure, we will not only experienced personal growth and prosperity but also became a beacon of hope and inspiration for others. This truth mirrors the principle found in Proverbs: **"Honour the LORD with thy substance, and with the firstfruits of all thine increase: So shall thy barns be filled with plenty, and thy presses shall burst out with new wine" (Proverbs 3:9-10, KJV).**

For **God's Mighty Men** to rise to their full potential, a shift in mindset is required. Instead of succumbing to murmuring and discontent, one should embrace the holistic principle of giving: dedicating time, talent, and treasure to the **Lord**. Such devotion promises not just individual growth but also profound societal transformation. As believers navigate the world's challenges, embracing this principle serves as a lighthouse, guiding them towards a life aligned with **God's** purpose. This alignment, marked by faith, dedication, and service, paves the way for blessings, prosperity, and **God's** divine favor.

A Spiritual Reflection

"Death and life are in the power of the tongue: and they that love it shall eat the fruit thereof." - Proverbs 18:21 KJV

Murmuring, or consistent complaining, is a self-inflicted wound in the spiritual realm. It reflects a heart discontented, a soul ungrateful, and a spirit misaligned with **God's** purpose. The Israelites, as they journeyed through the wilderness, were no strangers to this act. As Scripture reminds us, **"And all the children of Israel murmured against Moses and against Aaron: and the whole congregation said unto them, Would God that we had died in the land of Egypt!" (Exodus 16:2 KJV).** Murmuring led them to wander for 40 years, missing out on the blessings of the Promised Land.

As highlighted, it isn't just murmuring about our church that hinders our spiritual progress; it can seep into every aspect of our lives, including our relationships. The Biblical command in **Ephesians 5:25 KJV, "Husbands, love your wives, even as Christ also loved the church, and gave himself for it,"** reminds husbands of the divine standard of love they must uphold. When one murmurs against his wife, he is veering away from this divine mandate. By consistently speaking negatively, we shape our environment and the minds of those around us.

Furthermore, the act of murmuring against leaders, especially spiritual leaders like pastors, is not only detrimental to oneself but also to those under one's influence. As it is written, **"Obey them that have the rule over you, and submit yourselves: for they watch for your souls, as they that must give account, that they may do it with joy, and not with grief: for that is unprofitable for you." (Hebrews 13:17 KJV).** A pastor represents a shepherd, leading his flock towards **God**. Discrediting or maligning him in front of others, especially impressionable minds like children, can lead them astray from the path of righteousness.

This is not to say that pastors or leaders are beyond accountability or are immune from error. But there's a distinction between holding someone accountable and consistently criticizing without the intention of edification. Murmuring is a heart issue. It's about the state of our souls and our relationship with **God**.

The solution to murmuring is found in **Philippians 2:14-15 KJV: "Do all things without murmurings and disputings: That ye may be blameless and harmless, the sons of God, without rebuke, in the midst of a crooked and perverse nation, among whom ye shine as lights in the world."** To shine as lights in the world, believers are encouraged to act without complaints, reflecting a heart contented in **God's** purpose.

God's Mighty Men are those who speak life, embrace gratitude, and uplift others. They understand the power of their words, recognizing that the tongue has the power to bring forth life or death. As disciples of **Christ**, it is essential to tread cautiously, ensuring that our words align with the teachings of the Bible, spreading love, hope, and encouragement. By doing so, not only do we pave the way for blessings in our lives, but we also become a beacon of light for others.

A Call to Holiness

In the annals of spiritual history, there have been men

who stood out as beacons of righteousness, resisting temptation, and showcasing the transformative power of faith. These men, often referred to as **God's Mighty Men**, are the epitome of spiritual strength and dedication. Their lives provide us with lessons on how to battle against the allures of the world, reminding us of the importance of purity, holiness, and unyielding faithfulness to the Creator.

It is said in **Proverbs 28:13, "He that covereth his sins shall not prosper: but whoso confesseth and forsaketh them shall have mercy."** This verse illuminates the importance of confession and repentance. Regardless of the form or magnitude, sins serve as barriers between us and the divine. To progress on our spiritual journey, we must address these obstacles with honesty and conviction.

Temptations are omnipresent – from lust, idolatry, to the allure of worldly pleasures. However, as it is written in **1 Corinthians 10:13, "There hath no temptation taken you but such as is common to man: but God is faithful, who will not suffer you to be tempted above that ye are able; but will with the temptation also make a way to escape, that ye may be able to bear it."** This scripture reminds us that **God** never abandons **His** children. **He** provides the means to overcome every temptation.

Lust, often described as one of the most powerful temptations, seeks to overpower the soul. Yet, **James 4:7** encourages, **"Submit yourselves therefore to God. Resist the devil, and he will flee from you."** By recognizing the presence of lust and actively rejecting its influence, we take steps toward reclaiming our spiritual strength.

Similarly, idolatry, or placing anything above **God**, is a grave sin. **Exodus 20:3** declares, **"Thou shalt have no other Gods before me."** This commandment is not just a call to worship **God** alone but a reminder of **His** supremacy and the place **He** must hold in our lives.

Sexual immorality, yet another profound trap for many, is addressed in **1 Corinthians 6:18-20: "Flee fornication. Every sin that a man doeth is without the body; but he that committeth fornication sinneth against his own body. What? know ye not that your body is the temple of the Holy Ghost which is in you, which ye have of God, and ye are not your own? For ye are bought with a price: therefore glorify God in your body, and in your spirit, which are God's."** This scripture is not only a caution against sexual sins but also a call to honor our bodies as temples of the Holy Spirit.

To stand as a **Mighty** man of **God** is not merely to resist temptation but to confess and rid oneself of it. Confession is not a sign of weakness but a bold declaration of one's commitment to purity. It's an assertion of one's desire to be sanctified and to walk in alignment with **God's** will.

To be among **God's Mighty Men** is a lifelong pursuit, filled with challenges and trials. But with each confession, each act of repentance, and each rejection of temptation, we draw closer to the divine. As **Psalm 24:3-**

4 proclaims, **"Who shall ascend into the hill of the LORD? or who shall stand in his holy place? He that hath clean hands, and a pure heart; who hath not lifted up his soul unto vanity, nor sworn deceitfully."** The journey towards becoming a **Mighty** man of **God** is, above all, a journey towards holiness, purity, and an unyielding commitment to the Almighty.

Transformative Power and Renewed Relationships

In the sacred scriptures, we often witness profound accounts of men and women rising from frailties, moving away from their transgressions, and drawing nearer to the divine through repentance and the Holy Spirit's transformative power. These accounts serve not just as historical testaments but also as timeless spiritual lessons for us.

The act of murmuring and negative confession is not new; in fact, it has its roots in biblical history. When the children of Israel were delivered from Egypt, they often murmured against Moses and Aaron. **"And the whole congregation of the children of Israel murmured against Moses and Aaron in the wilderness:" (Exodus 16:2, KJV).** Such acts manifest a spirit of discontent, ungratefulness, and doubt. These murmurs are negative confessions that stand as barriers between man and **God's** abundant grace.

The recognition of this shortcoming and the fervent desire to break the habit is a testament to one's spiritual journey. In a plea for transformation, the psalmist once said, **"Let the words of my mouth, and the meditation of my heart, be acceptable in thy sight, O LORD, my strength, and my redeemer." (Psalms 19:14, KJV).** Here lies a plea for one's speech to reflect the love, appreciation, and gratitude for the Almighty and fellow beings.

The Holy Spirit's fresh anointing cleanses, empowers, and reshapes the believer. **"But ye shall receive power, after that the Holy Ghost is come upon you:" (Acts 1:8, KJV).** The believer, through this anointing, finds the strength to speak with appreciation, gratitude, and positive affection.

In communal worship, believers are often encouraged to share their experiences, testimonies, and transformational encounters. Such sharing not only strengthens the individual's conviction but also edifies the entire community. As stated in **James 5:16, KJV: "Confess your faults one to another, and pray one for another, that ye may be healed. The effectual fervent prayer of a righteous man availeth much."**

Many of **God's Mighty Men** faced challenges, but through divine intervention and their unwavering faith, they overcame. The trials faced by many - thinking of divorce or battling inner demons - are relatable. Yet, it's in these moments of challenge that **God's** touch has the profoundest impact, just as it did for men in Texoma.

Hallelujahs and praises arise when one witnesses the transformative power of **God** in action, renewing relationships, breaking the chains of negativity, and establishing new bonds based on love, appreciation, and mutual respect.

In , the journey of **God's Mighty Men** is a testament to the transformative power of the Holy Spirit. When faced with murmuring, negative confessions, and challenges, the divine intervention and the believer's unwavering faith lead to renewal and reformation. These experiences, shared among brethren, not only reinforce personal convictions but also uplift the entire community, bringing everyone closer to **God's** glory.

Embracing Spiritual Victory and Financial Health

In our pursuit of spiritual understanding, it is crucial to acknowledge the power of confession and commitment. This isn't merely a journey for the individual, but one that requires the fellowship and mutual support of our brethren. As the scripture tells us in **James 5:16 (KJV):**

"Confess your faults one to another, and pray one for another, that ye may be healed. The effectual fervent prayer of a righteous man availeth much."

When **God's Mighty Men** walk in unity and testify to the spiritual victories achieved in their lives, they acknowledge the transformative power of **God's** grace. Many of us have experienced the sheer might of the Holy

Spirit in breaking chains in our lives, be it the grip of sins, the allure of pornography, or the seductive whispers of murmuring and doubt. And when these victories are shared, they become testimonies to **God's** enduring love and might.

However, shedding one's past isn't merely about discarding the old but about embracing the new with all its promises. The transformational power of **Christ** is beautifully illustrated in **2 Corinthians 5:17 (KJV):**

"Therefore if any man be in Christ, he is a new creature: old things are passed away; behold, all things are become new."

Shedding the old tattered robe for a new, pristine one signifies this very transition from the old life of sin to the new life in **Christ**.

In our quest for spiritual depth, we cannot overlook the profound bond of brotherhood that the scripture celebrates. David and Jonathan's love stands out as a testament to the masculine camaraderie, a love so deep that it's said in 1 **Samuel 18:1 (KJV):**

"And it came to pass, when he had made an end of speaking unto Saul, that the soul of Jonathan was knit with the soul of David, and Jonathan loved him as his own soul."

It's a love that goes beyond societal understanding and is grounded in spiritual unity.

One can't delve into the concept of **God's** blessings without addressing financial prosperity. The call isn't for wealth for the sake of materialism, but for financial health as an extension of **God's** favor in all spheres of life. **3 John 1:2 (KJV)** underscores this very sentiment:

"Beloved, I wish above all things that thou mayest prosper and be in health, even as thy soul prospereth."

God's plan isn't poverty or riches but a wholesome life where our spiritual and financial aspects align with **His** will.

In , being **God's Mighty Men** is not just about personal spiritual achievements but about fostering a community that testifies to **God's** miraculous workings in their lives. Whether it's overcoming personal trials, forming deep bonds of brotherhood, or walking into financial health, the journey is underpinned by the unchanging love and favor of **God**. Embracing this journey with open arms and a committed heart ensures that we not only achieve personal victory but also inspire others to walk in **God's** glorious light.

God's Mighty Men and the Power of Obedience

In the realm of spirituality, the physical aspects of life, such as wealth and poverty, often become topics of intense discussion and reflection. As believers, we navigate the tumultuous seas of these discussions by focusing not on the outer markers of success or failure but on the inner markers of spirituality and obedience.

In the book of Proverbs, it's written, **“Better is a little with righteousness than great revenues without right” (Proverbs 16:8, KJV).** This scripture underscores the timeless truth that one's spiritual standing before **God** is not determined by worldly riches or poverty, but by righteousness and obedience to **His** word.

The key to unlocking **God’s** favor and blessing is obedience. The scripture from **1 Samuel 15:22** becomes the focal point: **“And Samuel said, Hath the LORD as great delight in burnt offerings and sacrifices, as in obeying the voice of the LORD? Behold, to obey is better than sacrifice, and to hearken than the fat of rams” (KJV).** This scripture not only emphasizes the primacy of obedience over ritualistic sacrifices but also reveals a profound spiritual truth: acts of sacrifice cannot substitute for acts of disobedience. No amount of giving, serving, or worshiping can compensate for deliberate disobedience to **God’s** commands.

God’s Mighty Men are not those with vast riches or those in abject poverty but those who have a heart to obey Him in all things. It's a call to evaluate our lives and see where we might be falling short, not just in the area of giving but in every command of **God**. Obedience unlocks the doors of **God’s** blessings, favor, and presence. For as **Jesus** Himself stated in **John 14:15 (KJV), “If ye love me, keep my commandments.”** The journey of spirituality is not about outward displays but about an inward commitment to obey **God’s** Word, and in that obedience, we find the true measure of **God’s Mighty Men**.

A Spiritual Exploration

"But be ye doers of the word, and not hearers only, deceiving your own selves." - James 1:22 (KJV)

As the Psalmist writes, **"Whither shall I go from thy spirit? or whither shall I flee from thy presence? If I ascend up into heaven, thou art there: if I make my bed in hell, behold, thou art there. If I take the wings of the morning, and dwell in the uttermost parts of the sea; Even there shall thy hand lead me, and thy right hand shall hold me." - Psalm 139:7-10 (KJV)**

However, even the best intentions can be marred by life's demands. There's an innate desire in us to "make up" for our lapses in obedience, to somehow compensate **God** for our perceived shortcomings. You cannot compensate by sacrifice what you have lost through disobedience. This principle echoes the words of Samuel when he reprimanded King Saul: **"Hath the LORD as great delight in burnt offerings and sacrifices, as in obeying the voice of the LORD? Behold, to obey is better than**

sacrifice, and to hearken than the fat of rams." - 1 Samuel 15:22 (KJV)

Many of us have faced moments when we felt **God's** nudge to act, to reach out, to share **His** love, or to embark on a divine assignment. But sometimes we delay, and then attempt to rectify it with a grand gesture. However, nothing can replace simple, pure obedience to **God's** calling.

Another profound kingdom principle shared is that prayer produces intimacy. This concept is akin to the sentiment expressed in **James 4:8, "Draw nigh to God, and he will draw nigh to you..." (KJV).** Prayer is not just a monologue but a dialogue, a deep and intimate connection with our Creator. It strengthens our bond with **Him,** with those we pray for, and those we pray with.

The essence of the spiritual life is not found in grand gestures but in everyday acts of obedience. **God's Mighty Men** aren't defined by their ability to make grand sacrifices, but by their willingness to heed **God's** voice daily. Their strength is derived from their intimacy with the Creator, an intimacy cultivated through consistent prayer and unwavering obedience.

May we all be inspired to be doers of the Word, cultivating a deep relationship with our Heavenly Father, and understanding that true spiritual strength comes from our intimacy with Him and our obedience to **His** call.

A Discourse on Obedience and Manifestation

When delving into the spiritual realm of understanding the Almighty and **His** teachings, one cannot overlook the profound significance of obedience. Obedience is not just a mere act of following commands; it is a testament to one's love, faith, and commitment to **God**. In this teaching, we will discuss the principle of obedience and its role in **God's** manifestation based on the teachings of John 14, 21, and 23.

I. The Principle of Obedience in John 14, 21, and 23

"He that hath my commandments, and keepeth them, he it is that loveth me: and he that loveth me shall be loved of my Father, and I will love him, and will manifest myself to him." - John 14:21 (KJV)

"Jesus answered and said unto him, If a man love me, he will keep my words: and my Father will love him, and we will come unto him, and make our abode with him." - John 14:23 (KJV)

From these scriptures, two essential truths are derived:

Obedience is the evidence of love.
God's manifestation is intrinsically tied to obedience.

II. Power and Obedience

The power of **God** is not a standalone force. It is intricately connected to the level of obedience displayed.

This concept aligns with the notion that **God's** power is released in proportion to one's obedience.

III. The Power and Presence of God

God's power and **His** presence are inseparable. To seek **His** power is to invite **His** presence. This union showcases that one cannot exist without the other, and to understand **God's** might, one must also be immersed in **His** presence.

IV. The Book of Acts: A Testament to Obedience

"And by the hands of the apostles were many signs and wonders wrought among the people; (and they were all with one accord in Solomon's porch." - Acts 5:12 (KJV)

In the Book of Acts, love isn't mentioned. However, the disciples and apostles exhibited their love for **God** not through mere words but through their unwavering obedience, even in the face of adversity.

"We ought to obey God rather than men." - Acts 5:29 (KJV)

V. Demonstrating Love Through Obedience

The greatest testament of love isn't through grand proclamations, but through steadfast obedience. It's in the everyday choices and decisions aligned with **God's** commandments where one's love for Him truly shines.

The narrative of **God's Mighty Men** is not only about their physical strength or their ability to wage wars. It is about their spiritual strength, epitomized by their obedience to the Almighty. In the world today, where love is often expressed in words and fleeting emotions, the principle of obedience reminds us that true love, especially the love for **God**, is showcased by our actions. The road to understanding and experiencing **God's** power and presence is paved with obedience. It is through our unwavering commitment to **His** commandments that we truly become **God's Mighty Men** and Women.

The Spiritual Act of Giving and Obedience

"For as by one man's disobedience many were made sinners, so by the obedience of one shall many be made righteous." - Romans 5:19 (KJV)

Throughout biblical history, men of **God** have been guided by principles that shape their relationship with the Divine. One such principle is obedience – a concept that is deeply rooted in the heart of spiritual matters. To understand the depth of its significance, one must delve into the teachings of the Bible and the expectations set forth for the believers.

As mentioned, "A ton of prayer will never produce what an ounce of obedience will." This statement, profound in its depth, draws our attention to the Book of Samuel where it is written: **"Behold, to obey is better than sacrifice, and to hearken than the fat of rams." - 1**

Samuel 15:22 (KJV)

This sentiment is reiterated when discussing the act of giving. The scripture underscores the importance of obedience in **God's** law. The act of giving is not just about money, it's about trust, faith, and a commitment to the principles laid down by the Almighty.

It's crucial to note the admonition, **"You reap what you sow."** This, of course, is reminiscent of the words of Paul in Galatians: **"Be not deceived; God is not mocked: for whatsoever a man soweth, that shall he also reap." - Galatians 6:7 (KJV)**

Some may try to compensate through prayer what they lose from disobedience hits home on the importance of following **God's** directives. When believers withhold their tithes, they not only deprive the church and the work of **God**, but they also deny themselves the blessings that come from obedience.

Indeed, the reasons for not giving as mentioned – unbelief, fear, and greed – all stem from spiritual shortcomings. It is written**: "Will a man rob God? Yet ye have robbed me. But ye say, Wherein have we robbed thee? In tithes and offerings." - Malachi 3:8 (KJV).** The act of withholding what is due to **God** is not merely a financial decision but a spiritual one.

In, to be one of **God's Mighty Men**, one must not only believe in **His** word but live by it. The spiritual act of giving and consistent obedience brings about blessings that cannot be compensated by mere sacrifice or prayer.

It is through these actions, grounded in faith, that believers align themselves with the divine principles of the Kingdom. Just as it is emphasized in Proverbs: **"Honour the LORD with thy substance, and with the firstfruits of all thine increase: So shall thy barns be filled with plenty, and thy presses shall burst out with new wine." - Proverbs 3:9-10 (KJV).** The true power and blessing come when we align our actions with **God's** will, honoring Him not just in words but in faithful deeds.

The Principles of Sowing and Reaping

Throughout the course of history, **God** has called upon **Mighty Men** and women to stand firm in their faith and walk in obedience to **His** commandments. These individuals, often driven by unwavering faith, have laid down their personal desires and have chosen instead to place the **Lord** at the center of their lives. One profound principle that has remained a cornerstone in the walk of faith is the concept of giving and the biblical teachings of sowing and reaping.

In the Bible, **Galatians 6:7** says, **"Be not deceived; God is not mocked: for whatsoever a man soweth, that shall he also reap."** This scripture encapsulates the spiritual law that underpins the very nature of giving and receiving, sowing and reaping. It reinforces the idea that when we give selflessly, especially in obedience to **God's** commandments, we stand to receive blessings in abundance.

Giving is not just a matter of financial obedience but is an act that touches the core of our spiritual being. **Malachi 3:10** states, **"Bring ye all the tithes into the storehouse, that there may be meat in mine house, and prove me now herewith, saith the Lord of hosts, if I will not open you the windows of heaven, and pour you out a blessing, that there shall not be room enough to receive it."** This passage speaks of the abundant blessings that come to those who trust and obey, emphasizing the magnitude of the favor that the **Lord** can bestow upon those who give with a cheerful heart.

Yet, some may ask, "Why is giving so critical to our spiritual well-being?" To withhold our tithes is to withhold a portion of our hearts from **God**. For where our treasure is, there our heart will be also (Matthew 6:21). This principle is not solely about the physical act of giving, but it's deeply rooted in our spiritual relationship with our Creator. To resist giving is, in essence, to resist a full relationship with **God** and can inadvertently lead to disruptions in other areas of our lives.

Many individuals, whether knowingly or unknowingly, attempt to compensate for their lack of financial obedience by sacrificing in other areas, such as increased prayers or acts of service. Yet, as profound as these acts are, they cannot replace the obedience **God** seeks when it comes to giving. It's a clear indicator of trust and submission to **His** divine will.

In closing, as men and women of **God**, we are called to

be exemplary in our faith and actions. The act of giving is a testament to our faith, an act that demonstrates our trust in **God's** provision and **His** promises. As we sow, so shall we reap. To experience financial favor, healing, and overall spiritual wellness, we must embrace the principles of sowing and reaping, starting with the obedient act of giving. May we always remember the words of **Proverbs 3:9-10, "Honour the Lord with thy substance, and with the firstfruits of all thine increase: So shall thy barns be filled with plenty, and thy presses shall burst out with new wine."**

God's call for **His Mighty Men** and women is clear. It beckons us to a life of faith, obedience, and surrender. Through giving and understanding the divine law of sowing and reaping, we align ourselves with **His** will and open our lives to the unparalleled blessings **He** has in store. Let our actions resonate with our faith, and may we stand as beacons of **God's** love, mercy, and favor in this world.

The Power of Faithful Obedience

Throughout the annals of history, religious texts and traditions have documented the unfathomable power of faith trust in **God**. It can move mountains, restore health, and create miracles. One of the most profound examples of faith in action can be found within the lives of **God's Mighty Men** – individuals who have dedicated their existence to living in accordance with divine commandments, often against overwhelming odds. This teaching will explore the transformative impact of unwavering faith, supported by scriptures from the Bible, that provides deeper insights into the spiritual journey of these stalwarts.

The Power of Repentance and Forgiveness:

"If we confess our sins, he is faithful and just to forgive us our sins, and to cleanse us from all unrighteousness." – 1 John 1:9 KJV

Faith is not just about obedience; it's also about recognizing our own shortcomings and seeking forgiveness. Through repentance, we acknowledge our sins and shortcomings, and through **God's** boundless mercy, we are purified. The prayer of repentance mentioned above captures the essence of this profound act. As believers utter each word, they immerse themselves in the ocean of divine mercy, confessing their misgivings and surrendering to the Almighty's infinite compassion.

Revelation through Praise:

"By him therefore let us offer the sacrifice of praise to God continually, that is, the fruit of our lips giving thanks to his name." - Hebrews 13:15 KJV

The act of praise is powerful. When one lifts their hands in worship and adoration, they are not only expressing gratitude but are also opening themselves to **God's** divine grace. Through praises, believers can experience a fresh anointing, renewing their faith and strengthening their spirit.

The Awakening in Men's Lives:

In this era, we witness an awakening in men's spiritual lives. A thirst for righteousness, a hunger for divine connection, and a yearning for spiritual fulfillment are evident. This rekindling of faith isn't mere coincidence; it's a testament to **God's** ever-present hand guiding **His** children back to **Him.**

"But the fruit of the Spirit is love, joy, peace, longsuffering, gentleness, goodness, faith," - Galatians 5:22 KJV

Men of **God**, in their renewed vigor, are becoming bearers of these fruits. They are the living proof of **God's** work, showcasing the transformative power of faith.

For the Glory of God:

"Herein is my Father glorified, that ye bear much fruit; so shall ye be my disciples." - John 15:8 KJV

God's glory is evident when believers become true disciples, living testimonies to **His** transformative power. Their lives, actions, and dedication serve as evidence of **God's** omnipotence and **His** promise of redemption to those who seek Him with all their heart.

God's Mighty Men are not just figures from the past; they are present among us, living testimonies of the profound impact of faithful obedience. Through their unwavering commitment to **God's** commandments, repentance, and steadfast worship, they exemplify the transformative power of faith. It's a reminder that no matter the challenges, with **God** on our side, victory is assured. These **Mighty Men** stand as beacons of hope, illuminating the path for others and showcasing the glory of **God** in its truest essence.

Spiritual Empowerment Through Faith and Unity

God's Mighty Men, as described in scriptures, epitomize not just physical strength but spiritual fortitude. It is evident from the passionate expressions of faith, moments of worship, and the encouragement for unity and love that these men possess an innate ability to inspire and lead. What makes them **Mighty** is not their physical prowess alone but their unwavering faith, their connection to the Divine, and their commitment to righteousness.

"I can do all things through Christ which strengtheneth me." - Philippians 4:13 (KJV)

The essence of this teaching is the transformative power of **God's** Word and the anointing of the Holy Ghost. Believers can attest to the profound impact **God's** Word can have on their lives. It not only brings about personal change but challenges believers to become better versions of themselves, more **Christ**-like in their actions, and more loving in their relationships.

"For the word of God is quick, and powerful, and

sharper than any twoedged sword, piercing even to the dividing asunder of soul and spirit, and of the joints and marrow, and is a discerner of the thoughts and intents of the heart." - Hebrews 4:12 (KJV)

The call to write a love letter to one's spouse is symbolic of the need to express love, seek forgiveness, and promote unity. It reminds us of **Christ**'s love for the church, his bride.

"Husbands, love your wives, even as Christ also loved the church, and gave himself for it." - Ephesians 5:25 (KJV)

Pastors, as shepherds of **God's** flock, require the prayers and support of the congregation. The act of laying hands and praying for the spiritual leaders signifies unity, love, and mutual respect within the body of **Christ**.

"Pray for one another, that ye may be healed. The effectual fervent prayer of a righteous man availeth much." - James 5:16 (KJV)

In, **God's Mighty Men** are not just historical figures from biblical times but are present-day believers who commit themselves to a life led by the Spirit, a life of unity, love, and righteousness. It is through the collective worship, shared faith, and consistent application of **God's** Word that they rise, conquer, and manifest **God's** glory in their lives. Today, as believers, we are called to be these **Mighty Men**, standing in faith, lifting each other up, and giving all the glory to **Jesus**.

"But ye are a chosen generation, a royal priesthood, an holy nation, a peculiar people; that ye should shew forth the praises of him who hath called you out of darkness into his marvellous light." - 1 Peter 2:9 (KJV)

To **God** be the glory, forever and ever. Amen.

ABOUT THE AUTHOR

Dr. Michael and Kathleen Yeager have served as pastors/apostles, missionaries, evangelists, broadcasters, and authors for over four decades. Havin authored over 260 books. They flow in the gifts of the Holy Spirit, teaching the Word of God with wonderful signs and miracles following in confirmation of God's Word. In 1982, they began Jesus is Lord Ministries International, Biglerville, PA 17307.

Some of the Books Written by Doc Yeager:

"Living in the Realm of the Miraculous #1"

"I need God Cause I'm Stupid"

"The Miracles of Smith Wigglesworth"

"How Faith Comes 28 WAYS"

"Horrors of Hell, Splendors of Heaven"

"The Coming Great Awakening"

"Sinners In The Hands of an Angry GOD", (modernized)

"Brain Parasite Epidemic"

"My JOURNEY To HELL" - illustrated for teenagers

"Divine Revelation Of Jesus Christ"

"My Daily Meditations"

"Holy Bible of JESUS CHRIST"

"War In The Heavenlies - (Chronicles of Micah)"

"Living in the Realm of the Miraculous #2"

"My Legal Rights To Witness"

"Why We (MUST) Gather!- 30 Biblical Reasons"

"My Incredible, Supernatural, Divine Experiences"

"Living in the Realm of the Miraculous #3"

"How GOD Leads & Guides! - 20 Ways"

"Weapons Of Our Warfare"

"How You Can Be Healed"

Made in the USA
Middletown, DE
01 October 2023